FRUITFUL
LIVING

FRUITFUL LIVING
by
Jessie Penn-Lewis

CHRISTIAN LITERATURE CRUSADE

U.S.A.
P.O. Box 1449, Fort Washington, PA 19034

GREAT BRITAIN
51 The Dean, Alresford, Hants., SO24 9BJ

AUSTRALIA
P.O. Box 419M, Manunda QLD 4879

NEW ZEALAND
10 MacArthur Street, Feilding

Originally published by
The Overcomer Literature Trust
England

Copyright © 1998
Christian Literature Crusade

This Printing 1998

ISBN 0-87508-946-1

Cover photo: SuperStock

Scripture quotations from:

The American Standard Version of the Bible (ASV),
   1901, Thomas Nelson & Sons, New York,
   unless otherwise indicated.
The King James Version of the Bible (KJV).
The Epistles of Paul (a translation and notes)
   by W.J. Conybeare, England (died 1857).

PRINTED IN THE UNITED STATES OF AMERICA

CONTENTS

BOOK 1

ABANDONMENT TO THE SPIRIT

Notes on the Book of Ezekiel

CONTENTS

"NOT YOUR OWN . . ."

"Ye are not your own . . . [but] bought . . ."
(1 Corinthians 6:19–20)

"The 'freeman' who has been called
is Christ's slave"
(1 Corinthians 7:22, *Conybeare*)

I'M but a slave!
I have no freedom of my own,
I cannot choose the smallest thing,
Nor e'en my way.
I'm a slave!
Kept to do the bidding of my Master!
He can call me, night or day.
Were I a servant, I could claim wages.
Freedom, sometimes, anyway.
But I was *bought!*
Blood was the price my Master paid for me.
And I am now His slave—
And evermore will be.
He takes me here, He takes me there,
He tells me what to do;
I just obey, that's all—
I TRUST Him too!

M. Warburton Booth

See Galatians 4:1; Philippians 2:7; Colossians 3:24.

BOOK 1

CHAPTER 1

THE LIVING CREATURES

The vision of the living creatures (chapter 1). Ezekiel prepared for service (chapters 2 and 3). Ezekiel used of God (chapter 4, etc.).

THE book of Ezekiel contains in it a wonderful picture of abandonment to the Spirit of God. Apart from its prophetical bearing, we may trace in it the work of God *in* a soul, and then *through* that soul as a pliable and obedient instrument in His hands.

The first chapter commences with opened heavens given to a soul prepared by God. Ezekiel was a priest, already separated to minister unto the Lord, but by circumstances was detached from his ordinary duties. At the time the "opened heavens" came we find him among the captives by the river Chebar in Babylon. He was the only one who saw these visions—because he was waiting on God in spirit, and it is only to souls thus still before the Lord that God reveals Himself.

"There," *in the midst of others*, the "hand of the Lord" was upon him, and the "word of the Lord" came expressly to His waiting servant, speaking to him not only in words, but, as it were, in picture-lessons, as a mother would teach her child.

First there was given to Ezekiel

THE VISION OF LIVING CREATURES

"I looked . . . behold a fire infolding itself, and . . . out of the midst of the fire . . . came the likeness of four living creatures" (ch. 1:4–5).

Scofield in his Bible notes says this passage of Scripture is highly figurative. The actual meaning of the "living creatures" cannot be definitely settled by any expositor. Spiritually, however, we may use the cherubim shown to Ezekiel as a Spirit-given picture of the new creation in Christ Jesus, born not only out of His death on the cross but out of the midst of the fire—*the fire of the Holy Spirit*. In the "new creation" pictured by these living beings we can trace the image of Christ as the "firstborn among many brethren." In the "eagle face" (v. 10) is suggested the Godward aspect of mounting up on the wings of faith and love in communion with God; in the "ox face" the patient life of obedience to the will of God; in the "lion face" the fearless boldness and the divine courage of the "faithful witness" (Revelation 3:14); and in the "man face" the perfect humanity of the man Christ Jesus.

Even so, when conformed to the image of the Son (Romans 8:29) we see that those who are new creations in Christ, born out of the fire of the Holy Ghost, have power to commune with God; they live in the will of God and have fellowship with the man Christ Jesus in His sufferings.

These "new creations" are also "joined one to another" (v. 11). "That they may all be one" (John 17:21) can only thus be fulfilled. Then "they went every one straight forward" (v. 12), "they turned not when they went." How this reminds us of St. Paul as he cried, "I press toward the mark," "this one thing I do" (Philippians 3:13–14, *KJV*). They "follow on to know the LORD" (Hosea 6:3, *KJV*).

In verses 15 to 21 we come upon the "wheels" as a marvelous picture of the life of the new creation in Christ, lived in full obedience to the Holy Spirit of God.

"Whithersoever the Spirit was to go, they went; thither was their spirit to go . . . for the spirit of the living creature was in the wheels" (ch. 1:20, *KJV*).

The Spirit of God in the wheels of circumstances, and the Spirit of God abiding and moving in the new creation, had no

friction between them, for "the *Spirit* was
. . . in the wheels," and the *Spirit of life
was in the living creatures*, therefore they
moved together in perfect harmony.*

This is a picture of life in the will of God.
God wanted to teach Ezekiel what it meant
to move in and with God, and God to move
in him. Trustful obedience to the Spirit of
God in him meant harmony with the Spirit
of God in the wheels of circumstances
working out "the counsel of His will"
(Ephesians 1:11).

Furthermore these new creations lived
and moved in the "terrible crystal" of God's

---

*This is blessedly true. A soul fully in harmony with
God, having no desire outside the will of God, is
always quickly *responsive* to the will of God in His
providence. Moving with God inwardly, there is no
difficulty in adjusting to God externally. This does
not mean that the soul thus in harmony with God's
will accepts all circumstantial "happenings" as His
will in *passive* acquiescence. The Spirit of God works
in a redeemed soul for the purpose of the *entire
renewal of the whole personality*, bringing every part
of the man, spirit, soul and body, first into fellowship
with Christ's death, and then under the energizing
of His risen life, so that he may become a fellow
worker with God (2 Corinthians 6:1), and not simply
an automaton passively acquiescent to His
workings. The *renewed* man then has perception by
the Spirit of what is truly of God in *circumstantial*
matters. He instantly moves with God in what is
clearly the "providence" of God, but he resists at
once what the Spirit of God in him plainly reveals as
of the Evil One. (Cf. Romans 12:2; 1 Thessalonians
2:18.)

presence (v. 22); they dwelt "in the light, as He is in the light" (1 John 1:7), with nothing between. The atmosphere was clear between them and God.

What do we know of this? When we live in God's "terrible crystal" there are no shady corners or "twistical" ways; no personal policy or tactics; no plannings or schemings; no deceptions or prevarications; no saying one thing and meaning another; no "end justifying the means" because it would answer our purpose. There is nothing that the world would use to reproach our God on our account, and which would not bear the searchlight of God.

When God had thus given Ezekiel the picture of the new creation abiding and moving in Himself, He lifted his eyes higher still—far above visions of what can be, visions of blessed possibilities—to Himself.

"Above . . . was the likeness of a throne . . . and . . . a Man above upon it" (ch. 1:26, *KJV*).

We shall never get to our right place—to the dust at His feet—till we get a sight of the Man upon the Throne (see Job 42:5–6). Paul saw the "glory of that light" (Acts 22:11), and from that moment said he counted "all things but loss for the excellency of the knowledge of Christ Jesus my Lord" (Philippians 3:8, *KJV*). Oh, may God lift up our eyes, that we may behold the

Man upon the Throne!

When Ezekiel saw Him, he fell upon his face. Then God spoke to him, and bade him stand upon his feet (Ezekiel 2:1). Apparently he could not do even this, until the Spirit of God entered into him and set him upon his feet—enabled him to get up and stand. With God's commands there is always included the power to obey.

This vision to Ezekiel shows us God's way of dealing with us. First comes the revelation of the new creation living and moving in the light and will of God, then He reveals the Man upon the Throne—the Glorified Christ Himself! Next we find Ezekiel at His feet as one dead, like John on Patmos, and the Spirit of life from God entering into him in deeper power to work out in him the vision he had seen. This is God's way.

HOW GOD PREPARES HIS INSTRUMENT

"He said . . . Son of Man, I send thee . . . and thou shalt say . . . Thus saith the Lord GOD" (ch. 2:3–4, *KJV*).

Now we come to Ezekiel's commission, and how he was prepared by the Holy Spirit for being used by Him, primarily as a messenger of God, next as a "sign," and then as a seer telling of things to come.

The very first condition was the interview with God, and the receiving of the commission "I send thee" (2:3). The second was "eating" (3:1) or receiving of the "roll" into his very being, ere God could say "Go, speak" (3:4).

This lesson is one for all who would carry the Lord's message. The question is so often asked, "How shall I prepare for this class, or meeting?" Here is the answer: "Eat—go—speak." "*Receive* in thine heart, and hear with thine ears, and go" (3:10–11). When the words are not "eaten" by the messenger, they fall powerless on the ears of the hearers. They must become part of the inner life, wrought into heart and character by the Holy Spirit, if we are to be true messengers of God.

Then again comes the glory of the LORD, and the Spirit of God laying hold of Ezekiel—lifting him up and taking him away (3:12, 14). He goes in bitterness and in the "heat of his spirit" we read, but in spite of this, "the hand of the LORD was strong upon me," he said. The next thing we see is that he is dumb, and again among the captives. He sat where they sat, and remained among them seven days (3:15), "astonished" at all he had seen and heard.

What a strange preparation for an obedient soul for special service. We would have thought that all that had occurred previously would have been sufficient equipment. What was God doing with His servant? At least we can see He was making him *pliable* in obedience, and ready for all He purposed to do with him as His messenger to Israel. First He says "Go," and when he obeyed and went where he was sent, then he sat dumb among his brethren, with nothing to say, till God gave him the message. This is the way God trains His messengers. What difficulty He has in making us pliable in His hands! Oh that our hearts were open to the Spirit of God as a leaf of a tree is sensitive to the breath of the wind (Isaiah 7:2)!

In Ezekiel's story we see how God prepares His children so that they may be pliable and obedient to the Spirit of God. When the Holy Spirit bade him go to the plain, he went to the plain (3:22–23), finding there the "glory of the LORD" so that he again fell on his face, and again the Spirit entered into him, *i.e.*, there was a renewed influx of the Spirit,* enabling him to rise to his feet, ready to fulfill any further commands from God. Now he is bidden, "Go, shut thyself within thine house" (3:24), and then told of suffering which he would have to endure at the hands of others, without a word of of approval, until once more God would give him the message which, when it came, had no reference to the indignities

---

* As with Peter in Acts 4:8.

the messenger had endured (3:25–27). This is true self-abnegation and absolute obedience* to the will of God.

And this is not all the testing God led Ezekiel into, so as to prove him in his surrender to the will of God, even as He proved Abraham. By sore experience Ezekiel had to prove that he was utterly yielded, even in family relationships, for when at the time of his wife's death (24:16) he is told not to weep, he did as he was commanded (v. 18). *Thus he did show also that he had learned*

---

*It is important to point out in connection with this implicit obedience of Ezekiel to the commands of God that there are passages in the book of Ezekiel showing that he did not fulfill these directions of the Holy Spirit as a *passive automaton* (*e.g.*, 4:14; 11:13). It is clear all through that Ezekiel had all his mental faculties in operation, enabling him to *know the will of God for him* in the matters referred to, and obey intelligently and deliberately. It is necessary to remember this, lest we conceive of Ezekiel's obedience as a subject obeys the mesmerist. Since this little book was first published in 1897, the Church of Christ has painfully discovered that there are counterfeits of true abandonment to the Spirit. We must take heed lest in fear of these counterfeits we lose the true. No soul can be fully used of God unless he becomes *intelligently* and volitionally obedient to the will of God. Note that Ezekiel had to *act* of himself in the sense that when the Spirit of God bade him "Go to the plain" he had to exercise his personal volition and go. It is necessary to remember this aspect of Ezekiel's obedience lest we imagine he had no intelligent part in voluntary co-operation with God in acting as he was bidden.

self-control in the most difficult realm of all—the realm of the affections. Oh, what it means to be obedient to God!

Again, in the giving of the message of God, Ezekiel had to be willing for the consequences according to the purposes of God, not the judgment of man. Once when he was speaking, a man died (11:13), and the heart-broken messenger fell upon his face, and cried with a loud voice, "Ah Lord Jehovah! wilt Thou make a full end of the remnant of Israel?" How painful to be a messenger of judgment. He felt as if he could speak no more, but the Lord sent him forth again.

It may be that we who speak of "full surrender to God" are too little prepared for giving up ourselves in reality to God to be under the hand of the Holy Spirit. We are too rigid, whereas He must have us pliable. We are so fettered by our "machinery," and say, "I cannot do my work unless I do it in this way!" and so He has to deal with us to get us out of our ruts. There is no freedom for the Spirit of God in cast-iron machinery. Let us not try to make others do exactly as we do, but help them to be what God can make of them individually. We would not like to see all our pots cast in the same mold, or a garden of flowers all of one hue. God gives every tree freedom to grow. May God keep us from hindering the work of the Holy Spirit in any of His children who are serving Him.*

Are we willing to yield ourselves to the Holy Spirit? Do we realize that we are not ready for service till we have met with God so really that we know we have received our commission from Him?

There is, alas, a vast amount of "Christian work" today that is not God's work—that is, work carried on by God Himself through human vessels. "*They* made me keeper of the vineyards; but mine own vineyard have I not kept" (Song of Solomon 1:6). Take care that *God* sends you, and then, whatever the apparent results are, it will be all right.

Let us look again at chapter 3:22–24. Ezekiel said, "The hand of the LORD was there upon me; and He said unto me, Arise. . . . I arose, and went forth . . . and, behold, the glory of the LORD stood there. . . . I fell on my face. Then the Spirit entered into me . . . and said. . . ."

God was able to work in Ezekiel so mightily because he was pliable and instantly

---

*Some "happenings" in the Church of Christ since this was written make it necessary to say again here that this does not mean our being "dumb" when we see the Counterfeiter misleading others under the guise of the Spirit of God. A soul as fully surrendered to God as Ezekiel was understands how to obey 1 John 4:1–4.

obedient to the Holy Spirit of God. See all through the story, from this chapter onwards, not the smallest resistance to the revealed will of God, or hesitation in obedience. God could count upon him to fulfill His will.

What a blessed picture of a surrendered life!

How few of us are willing for this utter surrender, this absolute abandonment. But the apostles knew it at Pentecost (see Acts 2:44–47), and if we are to know the real power of Pentecost it can only be upon these conditions—*all private interests and personal considerations utterly merged in the interests of God and of His kingdom.*

If God has turned His hand upon us in circumstances we do not understand to test our surrender and obedience, may we obey and trust implicitly our faithful God.

HOW GOD USED EZEKIEL

1. *As a "Sign"* (ch. 4:3). We have seen how the three first chapters of the book of Ezekiel are taken up with the revelation of God to Ezekiel, and then His preparation of him for service. The Spirit of God entered into him, to work within him in accordance with the purposes of God. We read that the Holy Spirit "took him up," taking him first to this place and then to the other, all to test and teach him how to be obedient to

the Spirit of God. All that Ezekiel did was to trust and obey the Spirit of God without questioning or hesitating. From chapter 4 on to the end, we have the story of God's work through Ezekiel.

Let us look at him now as a "sign." See how implicitly he obeyed God. A "sign" is always "speaking," even unknowingly to itself. Are we "signs and wonders"? Pentecost is always followed by "signs and wonders." David knew more about being a "sign and wonder" than many children of God now; he said "I am as a wonder unto many." Again see Zechariah 3:8 (*KJV*), "They are men wondered at," and again Isaiah 8:18, "Behold, I and the children whom Jehovah hath given me are for signs and for wonders."

Ezekiel was a "sign" to Israel as he showed his willingness to suffer for his Lord. He was a "sign" in showing that his household goods belonged to God. He was a "sign," and is a "sign" to us, in the way he ate his food. How many of God's children are in bondage in these areas? Surely we become a "sign" of grace when there is no grumble over these matters in daily life, because the body is manifestly under control.

God dealt with Ezekiel on every point: loosing him from his religious prejudices (4:8–17), and from bondage regarding food

(4:9–11). His body was evidently not his master, or it would have been hard to eat "by measure." He was loosed from pride of appearance (5:1); his property was at God's disposal: when God told him to prepare his belongings for removing (12:3), he did not say, "I like this place best." We say, "such a nice church and Christian fellowship!" or "I cannot move at an hour's notice!" How comfortable we make our nests, and think, like Job, that we shall die in them!

Again we look at him in chapter 21, as a melted soul! The word of the Lord came to Ezekiel saying, "Sigh therefore . . . with the breaking of thy loins [*i.e.*, a broken heart] and with bitterness shalt thou sigh before their eyes" (v. 6). "Cry and wail, son of man . . . smite therefore upon thy thigh" (v. 12). How ashamed people are of a tear! How reserved and unapproachable many of God's children are. Transparency comes after contact with God. If a past experience will help to remove another's difficulties, when utterly yielded to God we shall not mind being laid bare at the keenest point of our heart-life to give that help. The devil hates testimony; he will keep our mouths closed if he can, and hearts will remain untouched around us. The Lord must break us. He must pour us out if souls are to be blessed. Jesus wept. His tears flowed forth for Jerusalem and for the sins of His people Israel. He wept with the sorrowing ones at Bethany. We need melted hearts, hearts that will sigh and cry over the burdens and sins of others.

Ezekiel was a "sign" when God took away the "desire of his eyes"—his wife—at a stroke (24:15–16). God knew the sorrow, yet He bade him neither weep nor mourn. This teaches us that only when we take things which are painful to the natural man in a way contrary to the world, by the power of the resurrection life, shall we become a "sign." Death of the body is *not* death to the child of God who has learned the death fellowship with Christ in His cross and His grave. Paul says it is simply "sleep" (1 Thessalonians 4:14).

2. *As a Prophet* (ch. 6:1–2). Look now at Ezekiel as a prophet—that is, one who makes known the will of God to the people. See him sent out with his messages of judgment to the "blind leaders" and to the "princes" of Israel. See how God bore witness to the word with signs following (ch. 11:13). God seems to have used him alternately as a "sign" and then as a messenger, while Ezekiel was obedient to His will— obedient, whether told to be dumb or to speak, to be used just as the Lord desired, in judgment or blessing. May all the Lord's children learn what it means to be wholly given up to God for His will, for *this is the*

normal life in God set before us in the New Testament. Ezekiel's path was abnormal, even in the days in which he lived—but described in the language of the epistles of Paul, and set before us in the life of our Lord when He walked on earth, we see that Ezekiel's obedience to God contains in germ the principles of the life every redeemed soul is called to live. For absolute obedience to the known will of God is a fundamental necessity if we are to be used by Him. For this we are bidden (Romans 12:1–2) to present our bodies as a living sacrifice, and not to be "conformed to this world." "Transformed by the renewing of the mind," it is possible for us, as well as Ezekiel, to provide what is that "good and acceptable and perfect will of God" for each of our lives individually. The outworking of this obedience we can trace in the disciples in the early Church. They were not bidden to become "signs" in the same manner as Ezekiel, but they were "signs" to the people of Jerusalem that the Christ they had crucified still lived. So with us today. We too may be "signs" of the reality of Christ in a way which God desires for this unbelieving generation. We, too, must be content to be used by God as *silent* witnesses (*e.g.,* 1 Peter 3:1), or as messengers, "holding forth the word of life"; in either case "a sweet savor of Christ unto God," both "in them that are saved, *and in them that perish*" (2 Corinthians 2:15–16).

CHAPTER 2

THE TEMPLE

The vision of the defiled temple (chapter 8). The cleansing of the temple (chapter 36). The valley of dry bones (chapter 37).

PASSING over all the details, and the chapter on the judgment of Israel's enemies, let us see how the further revelation of God to Ezekiel can be applied to the spiritual history of the soul.

THE DEFILED TEMPLE

"Son of man, seest thou what they do? . . . that I should go far off from My sanctuary?" (ch. 8:6).

In chapter 8 God shows Ezekiel His defiled temple, and how He has to withdraw from the threshold, because of the sins of Israel. Is this a message from God to some of us? Does God see in us "idols," "the image . . . which provoketh to jealousy" (v. 3)? Does He see sin in the inner sanctuary of the heart? In the "chambers of imagery" (v. 12)? Is the imagination wrong? Is there

27

sin in our worship (v. 16)? Sin in weeping for the loss of our pleasant things, rather than for grieving God (v. 14)? Has God revealed idols in your heart? Are they put away? Are you *willing* for them to be put away?

See again chapter 14. Ezekiel was sitting in his house, with the elders gathered before him, waiting for him to speak. Ezekiel sat looking at them, waiting for the word from the Lord. As he waited God revealed to him the condition of the men before him. He was taken hold of by God and given His message. The Lord bade him to tell them about their hidden sins, and asks, *"Should I be inquired of at all by them?"* (v. 3). He said they must turn from idols if they would hear His voice.

Is it not often the same now? Christians gather to hear God's word. The speaker is fettered in giving the message. The Lord says, *"Idols! Idols! Let them turn from them, and I will speak."* Today, if anyone has an idol, or unsurrendered thing, let it go; no one will ever be truly blessed until the idols are gone.

God meets His people, and teaches them on the one condition *that they have no part with sin.* God has shown this to be possible. Look at God's promises of deliverance in Ezekiel 36:25–31.

"And will I sprinkle clean water upon you, and ye shall be clean: from all your filthiness, and from all your idols, will I cleanse you" (36:25).

"*All* your idols," "*all* your iniquity," "*all* your uncleannesses," "*all* your filthiness," "from *all* will I cleanse you." God can cleanse the heart. The blood of Christ avails. If you are willing to surrender all, God is willing to do His part and deliver you. See the promise of a "new heart," and a "new spirit" (v. 26). Do we each know personally this deep inward cleansing?

God shows the defilement and the heart idolatry in chapters 8 and 14, then in chapter 36 He shows us His remedy. All through it is "I will," "I will," "I will." It is *God* undertaking to cleanse His defiled temple. Have we trusted Him to do it? "Thus saith the Lord GOD, I will yet for this be inquired of . . . to do it for them" (v. 37, *KJV*).

Following heart cleansing, and the blessed "Garden of Eden" experience, there comes to Ezekiel the vision typifying death and resurrection.

THE VALLEY OF DRY BONES

"The hand of the LORD . . . set me down in the midst of the valley which was full of bones . . . lo, they were very dry" (Ezekiel 37:1–2, *KJV*).

How does this apply to us spiritually?

Apart from its teaching of the power of prayer, its primary reference to Israel and its blessed lesson about power in service, what is the spiritual meaning to a soul as it follows the chapter on cleansing and fruitfulness? In picture-lesson it can teach us fellowship with Christ in His death and resurrection. After the Lord has cleansed the heart He deals experientially with the perverted life of nature.* Objectively *in Christ*, the work is done, *we have died in Him* (Romans 6:1–13), but the Spirit of God must bring us into full conformity with His death, and the vision of bones, "very dry," pictures the experience of the believer when brought to the position of death with Christ. Just in proportion as this is actually wrought in us, the Spirit of Life in Christ Jesus will quicken us into vital union with the Risen Lord.

I remember once hearing it put so clearly by one of God's messengers. He drew a small circle to represent the heart, and this lay in the center of a large circle, represent-

---

*This has been described thus: "The life of nature is the life of the soul, deformed, perverted and poisoned in all its extent, in its foundations and its streams, in its roots and its branches. In the life of nature everything *runs to excess*. That which is good in itself is vitiated in its inordinate action. The natural life is always weak, selfish, inconsistent, changeable."—Professor Upham in *The Hidden Life*.

ing the whole man. God first lays hold of the center of the man, cleanses the heart, and takes the throne; then when the Holy Spirit is in possession of the *heart* He applies the death of Christ to the whole of the man, and makes room for His life from center to circumference. If you go on yielding to His blessed working, saying "Yes" to God in all the daily circumstances, your whole spirit, soul and body will become God-possessed and under the control of the Holy Spirit dwelling in your spirit. No hindrance now to stop the flow of His life and the fragrance of His presence ever reaching to all around, in love and peace and joy.

We are glad to have the grosser forms of self nailed to the cross, but the Lord desires to get us where the whole of our personality is possessed by Him. We can know *immediate* deliverance from the power of sin, but it is only as we yield continuously to the Holy Spirit day by day that He can bring us into full conformity to Christ in His death and resurrection.

The last thing that we contend for is our *spiritually-religious self*. We fight desperately hard to keep an *experience*, but to die means to let everything go, for in death we can hold on to nothing. It is then that we become pliable as Ezekiel was pliable, with no desires outside the will of God. We have nothing left to fight for. We die to our religious views, our old ways and habits of thought, our certain methods of action, and even all the *conscious* experiences of the presence of God, so that we possess God Himself rather than gifts from God. We surrender the "gift" for the Giver.

But when we have surrendered all, *He returns all*, purified and held in Himself for Himself. As long as we wanted to keep even a "blessed experience," there was a mist between the soul and God. If we surrender even the *manifested* presence of God, we become rooted and fixed in GOD. Not that He wants to take all away, but He wants us to *surrender*, that He might reveal Himself as an abiding reality. All is now stilled, all tossing over, and the soul calm in God. May He teach us what this means, and reveal Himself to the stilled soul! Yes, even the Bible may seem to be a sealed book for a time, and prayer becomes difficult, until we learn to sit silent at His feet and wait for Him to speak.

If God is taking any of us through this "valley of deep darkness" (Psalm 23:4, m.), let us trust Him in the dark (Isaiah 50:10). Do not try to understand, but say, "Lord, I trust Thee to reveal Thyself, to open the Scriptures to me, to teach me to pray." Let everything pass from you that does not touch your *personal* need. Do not make any *effort* to grasp "truth" and to take it in through your mind, but let God reveal to you all He wants you to know, and leave the rest.

Let us see, in the picture lesson, how God can meet the "dried-up" souls that He Himself has been getting ready by bringing them into this condition.

The messenger, carried in the Spirit, prophesies, *"O ye dry [souls], hear the word of the LORD."* Look over the valley; what a picture of helplessness, silence, death. Then there comes a "noise," a shaking (v. 7); the living Word causes the movement. Ezekiel looked on and beheld that "the sinews and the flesh came up upon them, and the skin covered them." He only gave the message, *God did the work*. This is a picture of real Spirit-service when God uses us, and not we trying to "use" God! When we *know* we have His message we can stand and dare give it, knowing that the Lord will confirm with "signs following."

The Spirit-sent messenger at His inner command now calls upon the Spirit:

"Come from the four winds, O breath, and breathe upon these slain, that they may live" (v.9).

Behold the wondrous scene, the blessed outcome. A resurrection army of souls brought out of death into life through union with the Risen Lord.

Now let us see the divine interpretation. We are not left to decide what this means. "Son of Man, these bones are the *whole house of Israel*" (v. 11). "Dried," "lost," "cut off." Primarily true of Israel after the flesh, how true about the spiritual Israel, the Christian Church; how true of individuals. God brings you to the place where you can say, "I cannot pray; I cannot take that class; I used to be such an active worker, but now I feel useless, stupid, helpless, with all my strength gone." Do you get a glimpse of what God is doing with you? He has brought to nought the "creaturely activity,"* that the energy of God may come into you in resurrection power and abundant life.

As God thus deals with you, you must take heed that you rely upon the blood sprinkled upon the mercy seat, to guard you *from the oppression of the enemy*; and that you do not give Satan any advantage by failing in your practical duties, and in the service of God. Maybe you are bewildered at what is happening to you. But see what Daniel was told about the promised Messiah. He was to be "*cut off*, and shall

---

*See footnote on page 30 describing the life of nature.

have nothing" (Daniel 9:26). God wants you to see yourself "cut off" with Christ in His death, "cut off" from the old life, the old strength and power (Ezekiel 37:11). Has He brought you to see the deep mystery of the cross, *that you have died in Him*? "*Cut off*" in Christ's death, *"cut off"* with Christ from your friends, from your old work, *"cut off"* from that blessed experience even of the "Garden of Eden"; all the fruitfulness apparently gone, the beauty, and the power. He is leading you on to know the Lord.

When the Lord Jesus died on the cross the Father hid His face from Him; it seemed as if He were "cut off" from God. Yes! it seemed so, and He cried, "My God, My God, why hast thou forsaken me?"

One of the last and keenest things to surrender to God is His *conscious* presence. We are ready to go through fire and water with the manifestation of His presence; but when this is surrendered all seems dark.

"Bones dried," "hope lost," "cut off"—this is the scene before us! Remember how the disciples left all to follow Him, but they recoiled when He spoke of the pathway of the cross. They could not let the Lord go to Calvary; they could not consent to lose the visible presence of their Friend. They could not understand His words, "I will see you again." Do you not see that when the soul reaches this point, there comes the WALK OF BARE FAITH? Cut off from yourself, from the old strength, from the old life, from old feelings, old companions, from dwelling in experiences, *to dwell in God*—this is God's purpose for you (Colossians 3:3).

Israel had come to despair. How blessed the word of the Lord, "I will open your graves" (vs. 12–14). Turn to a few other passages to illustrate this. See Job 19:6–21. See how David cried that he was "cut off" (Psalm 88:5–16). Then Jonah (Jonah 2:1–6), and Isaiah also, "I am cut off" (Isaiah 6:5, m.).

God brings the soul to this point, but He does not leave it there. He is working to an end. He gives the message of life, *"Ye shall live"* (v. 14). God interprets the vision: God will open your graves and bring you out. Then *"Ye shall know!"*

It is suggestive that we next see the story of the *joining of the two sticks* made one in the prophet's hand (Ezekiel 37:16–22). On resurrection ground there is union and oneness in God between His children. They are joined together in the risen life of Jesus. All divisions point to some degree of the carnal life (1 Corinthians 3:3–4). All divisions end in the grace of Jesus: there can be no friction there. All "walls of partition" between members of Christ's Body, even through external religious ordinances, are done away by the cross (see Ephesians 2:11–18).

Now let us sum up these lessons for practical use. Here we are a band of Christians. Are any "captives" here? Any not set free? We are here to get "visions of God," and the Lord has His eyes on those who are *seeking God alone*. He is here to set them free. Are you willing for Him to teach you? As we sit here, does the word come "expressly" unto you? In your will does He find *absolute surrender?* Surrender is not talk. There is a fashion of talking about the will of God, even when we are all the time *striving to make our will* the will of God! This is not true surrender. He will put you to the test. Surrender is not *dictating to God*. Circumstances will show us, if we are willing to see, how far our will is yielded to God. We see the sad effects of self-will in our work. How much of our Christian work is marred through special friendships, special likes or dislikes. "I cannot work with so and so." "I cannot do this or that"—self, not God's will, is ruling.

"Absolute surrender" means ANYTHING THAT GOD WILLS IN LIFE OR DEATH. When He sees us truly surrendered there is no delay in God taking possession. Will you have faith in the faithful God? Faith to believe that He is doing in you the work He undertakes to do?

Let us note here that the Spirit of God does not turn us into stones. He takes away the "stony" heart, to bring us out of the old life into a glorious life, the new life, full of resurrection power—with a heart of compassion and love shed abroad by the Holy Ghost.

Turn again to the vision of the valley: "They lived, and stood upon their feet, an exceeding great army" (v. 10 with 14). Let us step out upon the warrant of God's word, speaking plainly of death with Christ—"*Ye died*" (Colossians 3:3). "*We who died* to sin, how shall we any longer live therein?" (Romans 6:2). "Reckon ye also yourselves to be dead unto sin, but alive unto God *in Christ Jesus*" (Romans 6:11).

May God bring into the life in Christ "an exceeding great army."

CHAPTER 3

THE SOURCE OF BLESSING

The glory-filled temple (chapter 43). The ministry in the inner courts (chapter 44). The outflow of the living waters (chapter 47).

FOLLOWING the promise of cleansing and the vision of the valley of dry bones, and passing over God's dealings with the enemies of Israel in chapters 38 and 39, we see God giving to Ezekiel the vision of the new temple and its dimensions.

Spiritually interpreted, and applied to ourselves, are not God's dealings just in this order? First, the heart cleansed and indwelt by the Spirit; then the believer brought into personally experienced fellowship with the death of Christ, followed by union with the Risen Lord in His life, and oneness with others on resurrection ground; then comes the vision of the New Temple.

God can now *build up the new man*, the creation, to be possessed and inhabited by the Triune God. Chapters 40 and 42 suggest a most beautiful picture of this. Then comes chapter 43, with the vision of the God of Glory taking possession of the wonderful building, whose pattern was all His own.

"And the glory of the LORD came into the house . . . the glory of the LORD filled the house" (chapter 43:4–5, *KJV*).

"Behold, the glory of the God of Israel came from the way of the east" (v. 2). "The glory of the LORD came into the house" (v. 4, *KJV*), just as when the tabernacle was reared: "Then a cloud covered the tent of the congregation, and the glory of the LORD filled the tabernacle. . . . The cloud abode thereon, and the glory of the LORD filled the tabernacle" (Exodus 40:34–35, *KJV*). "The house was filled with a cloud, even the house of the LORD; so that the priests *could not stand to minister by reason of the cloud*: for the glory of the LORD had filled the house of God" (2 Chronicles 5:13–14, *KJV*). So it is with the individual souls; there must be the preparation of the new temple for the God of Glory to possess and fill.

The vision of God in complete possession is followed by the revelation of the priesthood acceptable to God, and their ministry within the veil.

THE MINISTRY IN THE SANCTUARY*

"They shall enter into My sanctuary, and they shall come near to My table, to minister unto Me, and they shall keep My charge" (chapter 44:16).

In verses 9–14, we see those who might not enter into the most holy place. "No *foreigner* . . . shall enter into My sanctuary." Nor "the Levites that went astray . . . after their idols," yet—the Lord adds—"they shall be ministers . . . ministering in the *house* . . . for the people. . . . They shall not come *near unto Me*, to execute the office of a priest *unto* Me."

Oh! solemn fact, no child of God with idols or uncircumcised heart can enter the inner court, although allowed *outward* service to "house" and "people." What a solemn word to us workers, showing that it is possible to be in outward active service and yet have no EXPERIENCE of entrance to the holiest of all. Those that may draw nigh are the obedient children: "they shall come near to Me" (v. 15).

How do they enter? See verses 17 and 18. Clothed with *linen* garments: *"no wool shall come upon them, while they minister . . . within"* (v. 17). Wool is a type of the natural or fleshy life; linen of the purity of God, of the robe of righteousness.

---

*See Ministry to the Lord, page 50.

Nothing unusual in their appearance is the thought that comes as we read verses 19 and 20. There is a tendency these days to label ourselves, to say by our dress or manner, "Stand by thyself, I am holier than thou." Pure linen from head to foot God commanded for His priests, and He commands us to have the inward clothing of holiness. This will be manifested in the humility and lowliness of Christ.

In verse 21 the Lord forbids all fleshly excitement. How many mistake *emotional life* for life in the Holy Ghost. He will give the true joy of the Lord if the heart is entirely separated unto Him.

In order to minister to the Lord we see, too, that He demands the utmost purity in all the lawful relationships of life (v. 22).

Verses 23 and 24 show us the outward service of the priests who enter the inner court. *"They shall teach My people the difference between the holy and the common."* They have power to discern what is according to the Word of God, and what is not; the difference between the life in the flesh and in the Spirit, between the carnal mind and the spiritual mind.

How subtle are the workings of the fleshly mind! How the children of God need sound judgment, and the guidance of the Holy Spirit. See the apostle's words in 2 Timothy 1:7 (*KJV*): "*God hath not given us a spirit of fear; but of power, and of love, and of a sound mind* [Greek: *sobering*]." The life in the inner court brings all three, and we need to see that we do not come short of them. Only in the sanctuary of God can we have clear discernment and be able to distinguish between things that differ. Let us ask for a sound mind, and power to discern the truth of God; then there will be God's rest in the heart, and His voice will be known. In verse 27 we read that the sin offering, the efficacy of the blood of Christ upon the mercy seat, is always needed, even for those who know the God of Glory in possession and the blessed ministry within the veil. "He shall offer his sin offering, saith the Lord."

Then comes the summing up of it all: *"I am their inheritance."* "No possession in Israel" (v. 28), for God is all in all.

Passing over chapters 45 and 46, how does the book close? What is the end and aim of all God's work in us? What is the practical outcome of being led on by the Spirit, from heart cleansing to the Spirit indwelling; from death with Christ to life in Christ? What is the outcome of the Spirit building within us the new man as a habitation of God? What is the outcome of the God of Glory taking possession of the totality of the man, and leading him on to know the ministry in the inner court? What is the outcome of thus going with Christ to the Father, and being hid with Him in God?

THE LIVING WATERS

"He brought me back unto the door of the house; and, behold, waters issued out from under the threshold" (Ezekiel 47:1).

The closing vision makes this very plain. The whole purpose of God's dealing is that living waters should be poured out in blessing to the whole world. We have traced the work of the Spirit within us, unceasingly leading us on and on in steady progression to the life of God. Now let us trace the *outflow* of the Spirit through the earthen vessel thus God-possessed and God-environed. God Himself is now the source within.

At the center the living waters begin to rise and issue from *"under the threshold"* (v. 1). Not an overflow, but an *underflow*; an under-current, deep, mighty, and strong, picturing the real power of the Holy Spirit, as it sweeps along like an overflowing river. How silently it rises under the threshold of the house, the stream unperceived at first, but growing deeper and deeper as it flows on. The vision refers primarily to Israel, and will be fulfilled in them literally in the fullness of time, but "rivers of living water" is the promise to all believers.

The prophet in a vision sees himself taken into the stream, first ankle deep, then on the bank again, one thousand cubits lower down, then back again into the stream, crossing it knee deep, then again back on the bank. Then the moment came when the *river carried Ezekiel:*

"The waters were risen, waters to swim in" (47:5).

When we have been really "immersed" in the Holy Spirit,* the stream of life may be only "ankle deep" at first, but the time comes when we, too, reach the "waters to swim in." This depends upon our obedient faith in God in the testing hours symbolized by Ezekiel's period on the bank of the river, for it is during these testing hours that the Spirit of God is deepening and purifying the channel. These times of apparent loss of the quickening stream allow, as a servant of God once said, the "silt" of the natural life to be removed, for a purer and clearer channel for the living water. The "waters to swim in" can only be realized when the soul has ceased to rely upon any support but God Himself, just as a swimmer must cease to depend on the upholding of the bank, to cast himself upon

---

*This is the real meaning of Acts 1:4–5. John's baptism in water foreshadowed Christ's baptism *in* the Holy Spirit.

the upbearing power of the water.

This was the vision that once came to a child of God as a picture of life in the Holy Spirit. She saw, as it were, a little straw floating on the ocean, borne this way and that way, sustained and carried by divine power. When the Holy Spirit thus has possession of a soul, with its full *reliance* upon Him, it must be borne along in spirit by His power. This is what we are needing. Let us cast ourselves upon God and hold Him to His word to make true to each one of us the very deepest fulfillment of "waters to swim in." Then He will be able to use us to the uttermost of our capacity for Him.

All this can be true, from the divine side, while, on the human side, the believer is fully exercising on his part "self-control," with his own volition of mind in full exercise—just as a man swimming in the ocean is borne and carried by the water, yet volitionally and *mentally* is consciously and actively co-operating with the power of the mighty waters bearing him along. Let us remember that "God-control" of a redeemed soul is manifested in the "self-control" of the man.

Oh, the activities of a life in God! Do you ask if it is an idle thing to let go all, and float as a straw on the ocean? Oh no!—the "floating as a straw" just pictures the *rest* of the one joined to the Lord *in spirit*. In the outer life of the body and mind the energy of God animates the whole being. The power of God energizes the soul for labors abundant, which are fruitful in the Holy Ghost. This is what is wanted for the mission field and at home. Let us see that the Holy Spirit has full right of way with us, and the fortresses of the enemy must fall.

If you know cleansing, and the heart possession by the Spirit, still press on. Let God bring to the cross your own life to make room for His. Has He brought you to this stage? Are you like Lazarus in the grave? Then listen! *He will bring you out.* What next? Be patient and believe that the wonderful, silent Operator within you is doing His work, silently building and bringing the new life to maturity. Then will come a fuller, clearer vision of the Triune God inhabiting the new man in his totality. Then deeper knowledge of ministry and union with Christ "within the veil," led step by step to the heart of God, to live in the world as a channel for God's life to flow through. Even here there is progression, for He leads on and on until the waters are risen—"waters to swim in."

Now return and see the effect of the river (ch. 47:7–12). "These waters . . . go down into the desert, and go into the sea" (*KJV*). The river flows on until it is merges into a sea until now devoid of life. "Everything

shall live whithersoever the river cometh."
Souls will be quickened wherever the child
of God goes. Rivers *flow*. So when the "rivers of living water" go out of you there is no
strain. Believe me, when you are possessed
by the Holy Spirit, lives around you must
be quickened. "Even so the Son quickeneth
whom He will." Christ in you will do the
work.

What a picture we have here in verses 9
and 10. *"There shall be a very great multitude of fish,"* and the fishers are all along
the banks of the river gathering in "exceeding many." Who can measure the blessing
of one day, when the rivers are running? So
great, so full, we cease to talk about it. How
many workers are satisfied if in twelve
months they see twelve souls saved! See
the picture here—*"a very great multitude of
fish."* This is *Pentecost*. This is what the
Lord has purposed for us quite as fully as
in the early Church.

What about "the miry places and the
marshes" (v. 11)? Marshes take in and
never give out. Alas, marshy Christians are
all around us, running about to all the
meetings, listening to and admiring the
preacher, yet utterly unchanged, and in
their lives remaining fruitless.

Next we see in verse 12 the fruit, new
fruit every month, not candied fruit, but
fresh and beautiful.

The book closes with four words:

"THE LORD IS THERE"

What lovely words! The cloud *abode* upon the tabernacle; the anointing which we have received "abideth." *"The LORD is there"* (*KJV*). Shall we let go our little efforts and press on through the path of the cross, into deepest fellowship with Christ in His death and resurrection until the river of God sweeps through us? Let us surrender self at every point and get to know GOD—God *indwelling*, God *enveloping*, God *surrounding*, God *carrying*, till the whole spirit, soul and body is possessed of God, and it shall be manifestly true in every point, "THE LORD IS THERE." O for the rivers, rivers, rivers! May the Lord do such marvels among us by the Holy Spirit's quickening and blessing that we shall become clear channels through which the water of life shall flow on and on; kept every moment in God; not satisfied with the blessing of yesterday, but living in God's eternal "today." Let us aim at "rivers." *Nothing short of rivers to swim in.* The river of God is "full of water." May we each become a free channel for its flow! Amen.

APPENDIX TO BOOK 1

MINISTRY TO THE LORD*

"Having . . . boldness to enter into the holy place by the blood of Jesus . . ." (Hebrews 10:19).

"AS they ministered *to the Lord*, and fasted," is the record given of that gathering of Christians in the early Church, when "the Holy Spirit said, Separate Me Barnabas and Saul for the work whereunto I have called them" (Acts 13:2). It is this waiting upon God until *God speaks* that we twentieth-century Christians know so little about.

We know much of:

> *Ministry to the "people"*
> *Ministry to the "house"*
>> (Ezekiel 44:11).

But little, oh so little, of that persistent waiting before God until we forgot our "necessary food"; until, like Moses, it can be said, "He heard the Voice speaking unto

---

*Written for *The Life of Faith* and given here as amplifying "The Ministry in the Sanctuary" on pages 41 to 44.

him from above the mercy-seat" (Numbers 7:89).

If the workers of today gathered together in this way to seek the mind of the Spirit of God, how different would the work be; and how quiet and restful would preparation for any meeting be, sure of its being in God's hands. There would be no making of programs and plans without *certainty* of their being "according to the pattern." Oh, that God's people might know the ministry *to the Lord* that will bring the *personal direction* of the Holy Spirit to those who seek and wait for it. Let us turn to Ezekiel 44 for a Spirit-given picture of this ministry in the "inner court" and its conditions and results.

THE SOULS WHO MAY NOT ENTER THE "INNER COURT"

Note first in verses 10–14 those who might not enter in person, although permitted to minister to "house" and "people" (v. 11). It is clear from verse 9 that all foreigners resident among the children of Israel, "uncircumcised in heart and uncircumcised in flesh," are automatically excluded from entering the sanctuary. *Levites*, however, who by virtue of their national identity are circumcised in flesh, are in another category. Though separated unto the service of God—"ministers" (v. 11), yet with "idols" in heart and life, and following afar off (v. 10); formally qualified but not cleansed from the love and desire of sin (which means that the knife had never yet been spiritually applied to the earthly, carnal life); unable to stand alone with God when the tide of worldliness or popular opinion would bid them compromise—*these* Levites, though admitted to serve manward in the sanctuary, must be excluded from priestly ministry Godward (vs. 11–14).

What a picture of many Christians today. "Workers" though they be, they may not, cannot, "execute the office of a priest" (v. 13) and minister unto the Lord in the most holy place. Busy, energetic, devoted, active in ministry to the "people" and "house," "they shall not come *near* unto Me," says the Lord.

"Workers," with idols in their hearts. "Workers," ordained to minister but serving afar off. "Workers," but under the power of besetting sin. "Workers," officiating in the energy of carnal life. "Workers," yet *compromising with the world* and fearing to stand alone with God.

THE SOULS WHO MAY ENTER THE "INNER COURT"

Contrast in verse 15 the Levites who were *true priests*: not only set apart for service, but cleansed, clothed and anointed for ministry in the inner court.

Of these anointed ones who had been faithful when Israel went astray from the Lord, God says:

"They shall come near to Me . . . minister unto Me . . . stand before Me . . . offer unto Me" (v. 15).

"They shall enter into My sanctuary . . . they shall come near to My table to minister unto Me" (v. 16).

And how are these cleansed, anointed ones to approach their God? Clothed (*head* and body) with linen garments (vs. 17–18). "Fine linen is the righteousness of saints" (Revelation 19:8, *KJV*). "*My* comeliness . . . upon thee" (Ezekiel 16:14, *KJV*). "Put ye on the Lord Jesus Christ" (Romans 13:14). Clothed with Christ Himself they enter in.

"No wool shall come upon them, while they minister . . . within" (v. 17). Wool typifies the carnal, earthly, natural life. This must be reckoned crucified upon the cross, that the soul may enter clothed in the divine life of the Risen Lord.

"One with Him, O Lord, before Thee.
There I live and yet not I;
Christ it is who there adores Thee:
Who more dear or who more nigh?"

THE OUTWARD LIFE OF
THOSE WHO MINISTER "WITHIN"

The ministry to the Lord means a *hidden* life. "When they go forth . . . to the people, they shall put off their garments wherein they minister" (v. 19). To outside people an *ordinary* life, in *ordinary* clothes, with *ordinary* language. No *outside labeling of inside privileges!* No peculiarity to call attention. Surely this at least is one thought given us in verses 19 and 20! Have we not missed God's pattern of the hidden life, and lived far too much "to be seen of men," ofttimes calling it "testimony"? Is there not the same thought in Matthew 6:17–18? "When thou fastest, anoint thy head . . . that thou be not seen of men to fast." Was not this the life of Jesus? Was there anything "peculiar" about Him but His humility, His calm, His words of grace, His life of ministry to others?

Again, in verse 21 we read, "Neither shall any of the priests drink wine, when they enter into the inner court." No fleshly excitement or stimulus can be permitted there. "In the MOST HOLY place" there can be nought but the deep hush and calm of the Eternal God. The Lord Jesus moved among men with calm dignity. "Recollected in God," the old saints would call it! Never hurried, even when the crowd would have hurried Him along. He had time always to do the "next thing" in His Father's will.

In order to "minister to the Lord" we see also that God demands the utmost purity in all the lawful relationships of life (v. 22), while ever and always needing the shelter of the blood spinkled upon the mercy seat. Cleansed, clothed, anointed, stilled, obedient. "In the day that he goeth into the sanctuary . . . he shall offer his sin-offering, saith the Lord" (v. 27). "Having therefore, brethren, boldness to enter into the holy place by the blood of Jesus, . . . let us draw near" (Hebrews 10:19–22).

THE RESULTS OF THE MINISTRY IN THE "INNER COURT"

1. *God is all in all.*

"I am their inheritance; . . . no possession in Israel; I am their possession" (v.28).

Nothing now but *GOD*. Lawful things, yea, even things given by God, "let go" for *GOD* Himself. Others in Israel may *lawfully* have these things, but those who enter "within" and minister in the inner courts find God their All in all. "No possession in Israel" (mark: not Egypt the world, but Israel!). Others might glory in what they had *from* God, these glory in having all *in God* Himself. "I am . . . thy exceeding great reward" (Genesis 15:1).

2. *Knowing the mind of God.*

"They shall teach My people the difference between the holy and the common" (v. 23), the difference between what is of God and what is not. The delicate intuitive knowledge of the will of God referred to in 1 John 5:20, descriptive of the Lord Jesus in Isaiah 11:3 (m.): "Quick of scent in the fear of the LORD." In the light of the Shekinah alone can many things be discerned. Things that differ in God's sight, yet *look alike* outside the "most holy place." Surely in these last days, when Satan is transforming himself into an angel of light, we need this clear vision to discover his counterfeits and his devices.

3. *Power to cause others to discern.*

"They shall teach My people . . . and cause them to discern between the unclean and the clean" (v. 23). Someone once said, "The Spirit *in* you makes Christ real to yourself; the Spirit *upon* you makes Him real to others." This is just the effect of the life in the inner court. How many who know much of the Spirit labor in vain to make others "*see* what they see." A deeper revelation of God's purpose for His children—not only *God in them*, but *they* "hidden with Christ in God" and made real in experience by the Holy Spirit—would enable them to "cause them to discern"!

4. *The mind of Christ manifested.*

"In a controversy they shall stand to judge" (v. 24). *"Without partiality"* (James 3:17, *KJV*) they see from God's standpoint; they are not influenced in dealing with difficulties by fleshly bias or fleshly prejudices. All prejudice and *partiality* is left outside the "inner court." "As I hear, I judge," said the Lord Jesus, "and My judgment is righteous; because I seek not Mine own will, but the will of Him that sent Me" (John 5:30).

Feeding upon the food provided by God (vs. 29-30), beholding the glory, and being "changed . . . from glory to glory . . . by the Spirit of the Lord," is it any wonder it is said of these who thus "minister to the Lord" in "the most holy place," that they "cause a blessing to rest on thy house" (v. 30)?

"Within the Veil": Be this, belov'd, thy portion,
Within the secret of thy Lord to dwell;
Beholding Him until thy face His glory,
Thy life His love, thy lips His praise shall tell.

"Within the Veil," thy spirit deeply anchored,
Thou walkest calm above a world of strife;
"Within the Veil" thy soul with Him united,
Shall live on earth His resurrection llfe.

FREDA HANBURY ALLEN

BOOK 2

MUCH FRUIT

CONTENTS

The Soul Winner's Secret

"If it die . . . much fruit" (John 12:24)

THERE is no field without a seed.
Life raised through death is life indeed.
The smallest, lowliest little flower
A secret is, of mighty power—
To die—it lives—buried to rise—
Abundant life through sacrifice.
Would'st thou know gain? It is
  through loss;
Thou can'st not save but by the cross.
A corn of wheat, except it die,
Can never, never multiply.
The glorious fields of waving gold,
Through death are life a hundredfold.
Thou, who for souls dost weep and pray,
Let not hell's legions thee dismay—
This is the way of ways for thee,
The way of certain victory.

M. WARBURTON BOOTH

BOOK 2

CHAPTER 1

THE STORY OF
A GRAIN OF WHEAT

"Except a grain of wheat fall into the earth and die, it abideth . . . alone, but if it die, it beareth much fruit" (John 12:24).

THE Lord Jesus Himself is undoubtedly the One referred to primarily in this passage, but He adds "If any man serve Me, let him follow Me" to call the "children of the kingdom" into fullest fellowship with Himself, so that in the laying down of life they too may bring forth much fruit to His Father's glory. Not, be it remembered, in the aspect of propitiation for sins, for *"He trod the winepress alone, and of the people there was none with Him"* (see Isaiah 63:3), but in obedience to the law of sacrifice for fruitfulness. Union with Him who gave His life as the first Seed-grain is essential to us His followers today, if we are to fulfill the purpose of our being.

To trace the early history of God's seed-grains, we must turn to the parable of the

Sower, the parable of "beginnings."

"He saith unto them, Know ye not this parable? and how shall ye know all the parables?" (Mark 4:13).

If we do not understand how the seed springs into life quickened by the Holy Spirit's power, and becomes the *beginning* of the life of God in the soul, how can we understand the development of that life, and the later stages of its growth, as they are put before us in other parables? How shall we be able to comprehend the law of sacrifice, as revealed in the pouring out unto death of the first Seed-grain? For true knowledge of the mysteries of the kingdom always *corresponds to the development of the hidden life of the kingdom within us.*

THE PARABLE OF BEGINNINGS:
THE SOWER, THE SEED AND THE GROUND

1. *"Behold, the sower went forth to sow"* (Mark 4:3).

The sower may be the husbandman Himself, or His laborers sent forth at His command. In either case we see that all seeking for souls, and all sowing of the seed of life, begins on God's side, with God Himself. "*God* so loved . . . that *He* gave" (John 3:16).

2. *The seed sown by the sower.*
"The seed is the word of God" (Luke 8:11).

"The word of the kingdom" (Matthew 13:19).

The written word contains the germ of eternal life. The Living Word, the Christ of God, is *hidden* in the written word; and when planted in the heart of man, a new life is communicated, so that souls are begotten "by the word of truth" (James 1:18). "Born again, not of corruptible seed, but . . . by the word of God, which liveth and abideth for ever" (1 Peter 1:23, *KJV*).

3. *The ground in which the seed is sown.*
"Some fell by the way side" (Mark 4:4, *KJV*).
"Some fell on stony ground" (Mark 4:5, *KJV*).
"Some fell among thorns" (Mark 4:7, *KJV*).
"Other fell on good ground" (Mark 4:8, *KJV*).

The same seed, containing the same life-germ, the same possibilities—yet meeting with four different results in four classes of hearers. Oh, how solemn is this parable of "beginnings." How much depends on the start!

THE SEED-SOWINGS

1. *The wayside sowing.*
"Those by the way side are they that have heard; then cometh the devil, and taketh away the word" (Luke 8:12).

That which lies on the surface is easily caught away. The devil comes to every seed-sowing of the word of life! He must be there to "immediately" (Mark 4:15) snatch the seed away, for the hearer must not be given time to think. What he fears is *"lest they should believe, and be saved."*

It is the *word of God* that he is keen to snatch away! Let God's messengers remember this. The devil is not afraid of addresses *about* the word, but of *the word itself* which contains the germ of life. Addresses may be so brilliant, or so voluminous, as to contain no real "seeds"; or else so scattered that they do not reach the ground of the hearts of the hearers at all.

2. *The seed in the stony ground.*

"Those on the rock are they who, when they have heard, receive the word with joy; and these have no root, who for a while believe, and in time of temptation fall away" (Luke 8:13; cf. Mark 4:16–17).

These hearers received the word with joy; their emotions were deeply stirred, but these joyful receivers had "no root." How could there be deep root unless the stony ground had been plowed, and the stones gathered out? The sower must not only sow the seed, but he must sow it in *plowed ground.*

The seed sown on these two kinds of ground apparently comes to nothing. The hearers have moved on—possibly to be reached again by some other sower.

3. *The seed in thorny ground.*

"Other fell among the thorns, and the thorns grew up, and choked it, and it yielded no fruit. . . . These are they that have heard the word, and the cares of the world, and the deceitfulness of riches, and the lusts of other things entering in, choke the word, and it becometh unfruitful" (Mark 4:7, 18–19).

Here the seed of life has really taken root, and sprung up. It is planted in the heart, but it has not room enough to permit its full growth. It is choked with (1) *cares*, (2) *riches*, (3) *pleasures*, or (4) *the love of "other things."*

Here we have a heart which has opened to receive the word of God, but which has never been cleansed in its desires, or wholly surrendered to God. Carnal Christians, fruitless Christians—what multitudes there are! They bring "*no fruit to perfection*" (Luke 8:14, cf. Rev. 3:2). They never reach the point of fitness to be God's seed-grains. There is fruit, in the sense that the little blade of wheat begins to show itself, but it is weak, feeble, stunted in its growth.

Can nothing be done to the thorny ground, even though the "beginning" shows a possible end of "no fruit to perfection"? Yes, thank God, there can, for other parables tell how God deals with unfruitful souls. The thorny ground may yet be cleared of its thorns, and the seed of life come to full maturity.

The prophet Isaiah gives us, in Old Testament language (and primarily spoken of Israel), a vivid picture of the way God must deal with the life which produces thorns:

"The Lord of Hosts . . . shall kindle a burning like the burning of a fire. And the light of Israel shall be for a fire, and His Holy One for a flame: and it shall burn and devour his thorns and his briers in one day; and shall consume . . . from the soul, and even to the flesh" (Isaiah 10:16–18, *KJV*, m.).

The thorns of earth which made a thorny crown for the Christ of God, and which will make a thorny path for us in following Him, must be burned. The meaning of this is simply—

"Receive ye the Holy Spirit" (John 20:22).

"God, who knoweth the heart, bare them witness, giving them the Holy Spirit, . . . cleansing their hearts by faith" (Acts 15:8–9).

How many receive Jesus the Saviour, Himself the gift of eternal life, who do not know that they may also receive the gift of the Ascended Lord—the Holy Spirit, the Comforter! How few know that the Holy Spirit comes to cleanse the heart, and to reveal in ever deepening reality the Christ of God! If the seed of life is to reach full growth, the Holy Spirit must be given entire control in the whole being.

"When the Comforter is come . . . He shall bear witness of Me," said the Lord

Jesus (John 15:26). The Holy Spirit will bear witness to the finished work of the Redeemer, and give a true inward knowledge of the cross of Calvary, furthermore revealing the Risen and Ascended Lord. He will purify the heart from its old desires, by applying the death of the Crucified One, and will make the cross a *continuous power* to separate from that earth life which produced the thorns, so that the heavenly life may grow within us to full maturity; for "the word of the cross . . . unto us who are being saved . . . is the power of God" (1 Corinthians 1:18, m.).

CHAPTER 2

THE STORY OF THE SEED-GRAIN

"That in the good ground, these are such as in an honest and good heart, having heard the word, hold it fast, and bring forth fruit with patience" (Luke 8:15).

L ET us now trace the story of the seed of life planted in good soil. The life with the most favorable beginning will come to maturity the soonest. Let us remember this, fellow sowers in the Master's service. *Let us aim at well-born souls.* Let us seek to do more careful sowing, so as to send the young converts out into the world handicapped as little as possible at the start. Nay, even more, let us remember that our own level ofttimes determines the level of those we lead to Christ. A feeble tree produces sickly fruit. Let the life be strong in us and it will be strong in those we win for Christ.

The Master describes the ground as good when it is honest! *"None is good, save . . . God,"* said the Holy Son of God!

"There is none that doeth good, no not one," adds the Apostle Paul. A good heart therefore seems to be an *honest* heart, honest with itself and God, honest in purpose to *know the truth* and to do it.

An honest heart will not try to cloke its sins, or use "circumstances" and "training" as excuses. It will not evade the truth of God and seek to "establish its own righteousness." It will cry out, "God be merciful to me a sinner," while others may be saying, "I thank Thee I am not as other men." It is honest with itself; it honestly desires to know the truth about itself, however humiliating that may be. It is honestly willing to put away sin, and to accept salvation on God's terms.

Honest renouncing of sin *because it is sin* will make good ground for the word of life, for many grieve over the consequences of their sin far more than over the sin itself in its exceeding sinfulness.

An honest heart "heareth the word, and understandeth it" (Matthew 13:23), because the Spirit reveals the truth when there is honest desire to obey it, for He will deign to teach a soul beset with honest difficulties while He refuses to satisfy mere curiosity. You may recall that Herod was hoping to see Jesus perform some miracle, and so he questioned Him at length; but *Jesus answered him nothing* (Luke 23:8–9).

Honest dealing with sin, honest renunciation of all known sin, honest confession of sin, honest desire to know the truth and to do it, honest reception of the word of God without reasoning; these conditions make good ground for the sowing of the seed. In such a heart the word of God can work effectually. In such a heart the seed takes rapid root, and the "word of the cross" will have full power.

Honest obedience, holding fast the word of God as revealed by the Spirit day by day, will lead the soul from faith to faith in steady growth. The Father is the Husbandman. He has sent forth His Spirit to take personal charge of the one who receives His Son, and He will faithfully do His work as the silent, unceasing Operator within.

THE GROWTH OF THE SEED OF LIFE

"Having heard the word, keep it [not hurrying it into forced growth], and bring forth fruit with patience" (Luke 8:15, *KJV*)

The seed need not be watched to see if it is growing! It need not be dug up to see if it has taken root! It can be left! *"So is the kingdom of God, as if a man should cast seed upon the earth; and should sleep and rise night and day, and the seed should spring up and grow, he knoweth not how"* (Mark 4:26–27).

It will do its own work, and conquer and

make room for itself, under the watchful care of the Divine Spirit. If the human sower is *purely the channel of the Spirit* in receiving the message and in ministering the word of life, the Divine Spirit will direct the seed into the right ground, and the sower may go his way. It can be left, for it will spring up of itself, and bring forth fruit in its season, *"first the blade, then the ear, then the full grain in the ear"* (Mark 4:28).

Patience is needed. Oh, the "patience of Jesus Christ"!

"The Husbandman waiteth for the precious fruit of the earth and hath long patience for it" (James 5:7, *KJV*). He is patient over the stages of its steady development, *"first* the blade, *then* the ear." To the little green blade, just shooting out of the ground, He does not speak of "falling into the ground to die." He is silent about this even when the green stalk appears, and begins to grow tall. When the green head (ear) of wheat is forming, and is preparing to become the "full grain in the ear," when still in its green, pulpy condition, it is far from being fit for sowing in the ground.

Patience, child of God! Learn to wait. Learn to give God time with yourself and others. "God . . . worketh for him that waiteth for Him." "Consider the lilies . . . how they grow; they toil not," but how *we* toil in struggling to grow! How heavy we make the burden of watching, and caring for our own soul.

Depend upon the Holy Ghost, oh honest heart—the Holy Spirit who is the breath of God—to breathe into you day by day and quicken and nourish the life He has planted in you. He will watch over His word to perform it, and bring forth the life eternal from blade to head, and after that the full grain in the head.

But—*"How far does He depend on me to co-operate with Him?"* is the question here! Just so far as to ask your utter abandonment to Him day by day, and implicit obedience to all the light He reveals. For it is true that

". . . you can go no faster than a full dependence upon God can carry you.

"God is always present, and always working towards the life of the soul, and its deliverance from captivity . . . but this inward work of God, though never ceasing or altering, is yet always and only hindered by the activity of our own nature and faculties; by bad men through their obedience to earthly passions; by good men through striving to be good in their own way, by their natural strength and . . . seemingly holy labours and contrivances."*

The divine Husbandman is satisfied with the blade of wheat at its proper stage. He

---

*William Law, *The Power of the Spirit.*

does not expect *it* to be "golden grain." Patience, patience, little green blade. "He that believeth shall not make haste."

Time goes on. The little green blade has left its growth to God and has almost forgotten about its growing, for it has just been trusting through the dark days, and rejoicing in the sunny ones when they came, accepting each from the Father's hand.

It has given up "toiling," and taken to trusting, when suddenly it awakens to find that it has produced a head filled with grain. It thought it would never produce some real grains, the growth seemed so slow! Then when the grains came they seemed at first so immature and so unfit for any use. The heads seemed all husk with no grain at all! Would it never be "golden grain"? it said to itself. Meanwhile the days went on. "The Sun of Righteousness" shone into the heart, and there came the rain of the Spirit from the Father, until at last the fruit was ripe. In the sunshine there sways in the breeze on the top of the stalk the full head of wheat.

THE RIPE GRAIN OF WHEAT

"Fruit, thirtyfold, and sixtyfold, and a hundredfold. . . . When the fruit is ripe, straightway he putteth forth the sickle" (Mark 4:20, 29).

Let us leave the group of grains—the "full grain in the ear" to which the seed sown by the sower has matured—and follow the story of one little grain of wheat out of the hundredfold.

The little grain of wheat finds itself one of many, all bound together in cosy nests on the top of the stalk. Such a happy group, living in the sunshine, rejoicing in the refreshing showers and the lovely summer air!

"Is this the end of it all?" we ask. "Is this the goal; is this the full purpose of its being?" If the grain of wheat could talk, we might see it looking down on the little blades of wheat just peeping out of the ground and hear it say, *"Come up here."* Or it might forget them altogether, and become absorbed in its own beautiful life "far above all," for it left all of earth when it grew up to its present position, and nothing concerns it where it is.

On the top of that stalk there is peace from the hullabaloo of society, separation from the things of earth, and happy fellowship with its own group of grains. There is only room for just the hundredfold in the head of wheat, and the little grain is apt to be limited to its own point of vision, and to think that no other "full grain in the ear" is quite like itself!

What a picture of many of God's children

who have followed on to know the Lord, and have grown up with others in happy circles and favored surroundings. How bright the days, how happy the fellowship, how delightful the meetings, the Bible readings, the service of God! How easy to look out from cosy nests and to pity less favored souls. How easy to become spiritually self-absorbed. *"Holy yet hard"* is the danger here, for it is possible to be a really sanctified soul but shut in and narrowed within our own limit; a *victorious* soul, but severe on others not on our level of experience. We may know how to "work for God," and yet lack that passion for self-sacrifice which would lead us to be poured out upon the sacrifice and service of others' faith like the Apostle Paul (See Philippians 2:17, m.).

IS THE HUSBANDMAN SATISFIED?

Is God satisfied? No, He has fuller purposes for the grain of wheat. It has not yet fulfilled the cause of its being. It has reached maturity, it is true—and hitherto the main purpose has been its growth, for it has been getting for itself and absorbing all the necessary nourishment that it might become the "golden grain"—but that is not its intended end.

There are now three courses open to the ripened grain of wheat:

1. *It may be gathered alone into the heavenly barn.* "He will gather His wheat into the garner" (Matthew 3:12).

Although sifted by Satan and tossed by sorrow and trial, the Father has promised that "not the least grain shall fall" (Amos 9:9). But to be one of the garnered ones in the great harvest of the Son of Man is not the fullest development possible to the grain of wheat. Yet how many place their own salvation, or sanctification, as the ultimate end of all their desires.

2. *It may be used as bread-grain.* "Bread-corn is bruised; nay, He will not ever be threshing it . . . He doth not crush it" (Isaiah 28:28, *KJV*, m).

The wheat that is gathered into the garner is separated from the chaff, but it is neither bruised nor broken, and both are necessary for the further use or development of the ripened grain. The Father's bread-grain must needs be bruised, but it is *never crushed* so as to be useless!

May this not mean *fellowship with the sufferings of Christ*, so as to be made "perfect through suffering," for "the disciple must be perfected as his Master"? (See Hebrews 2:10, Luke 6:40).

3. *It may become one of the seed-grains, bringing forth much fruit.* "Except a grain of wheat fall into the earth and die, it abideth by itself alone; but if it die, it beareth much fruit"

(John 12:24). "That which thou thyself sowest is not quickened except it die" (1 Corinthians 15:36).

The *bruised* bread-grain and the *buried* grain of wheat may be but two aspects of God's working for bringing the "life of God in the soul of man" into the fullest development for His eternal glory.

The *bruised* bread-grain may speak of the *Godward aspect*, as the threshing brings conformity to the image of Christ. The "bread of . . . God" in the holy place (Leviticus 21:21) signified the character of Jesus, and His perfect acceptance by the Father as the One in whom He was well-pleased. It is also written that *"we, who are many, are one bread, one body"* (1 Corinthians 10:17). The bread is composed of many grains of wheat, ground and knit together by fire to form *one loaf.* Thus are we joined to Christ our Head; and in Him and with Him, in the holy place, do we become the "bread of God" (John 6:33), accepted in the Beloved.

The *buried* grain may speak of the *manward aspect* of the breaking forth of the divine life from the broken grain, even as it is written, *"Death worketh in us, but life in you"* (2 Corinthians 4:12). This seems to point to the being poured out upon the sacrifice and service of the faith of others—the selflessness of self-forgetfulness that others may be blessed.

To see the way the Husbandman brings this about, let us pass on to the history of the buried seed-grain.

> On the way to the garner,
> Its death is life from another.
> Willing to die, willing to go,
> Never been taught to answer No!
> Leave the fields for others, to die;
> "Faithful to Thee," its deepest cry . . .
> Then take me and use me, and
>   crush me to dust;
> Thy hand and Thy heart I'll
>   faithfully trust.

EVAN ROBERTS

CHAPTER 3

THE BURIED SEED-GRAIN

"Another parable put He forth unto them. . . . He that soweth the good seed is the Son of Man; the field is the world; the good seed are the children of the kingdom" (Matthew 13:24, 37–38, *KJV*).

HERE we have another sowing quite distinct from the sowing of the seed of the *Word*. The sowing of the "children of the kingdom" in the "field of the world," by the Son of Man Himself, is expressly stated.

The sowing of the *seed-grains*—those produced from the sowing of the seed of the Word in the good ground and coming to full maturity in the "ear"—is now spoken of. The Master uses His laborers to sow the word of life, but each seed-grain He takes into *His own* pierced hands; He can trust it to no other, and He says, *"I will sow her unto Me in the earth"* (Hosea 2:23). "Her"— *whom?* The one He has allured into the wilderness. The one He has drawn away from all of earth to hear Him say, "I will betroth thee unto Me in righteousness . . . and thou shalt know the LORD" (Hosea 2:19–20, *KJV*). The one joined to the Lord, who is the *first* Seed-grain.

"It shall come to pass in that day ["that day . . . that thou shalt call Me *Ishi*," vs. 16], I will answer, saith Jehovah, I will answer the heavens, and they shall answer the earth; and the earth shall answer the grain, and the new wine, and the oil; and they shall answer Jezreel ['whom God soweth']. And I will sow her unto Me in the earth" (Hosea 2:21–23).

The Creator responds to the desire of the heavens, and commands it to pour out its blessing on the earth. The heavens respond to the cry of the earth by giving the early and latter rain. Whereupon the earth responds to the grain and new wine and oil by giving them forth in abundant measure. Heaven and earth unite in responding to the will of the Creator for the buried seed-grain "whom God soweth."

Then it shall come to pass through the yielded life of the soul in union with its Lord—

"I will say to them that were not My people, Thou art My people; and they shall say, Thou art my God" (Hosea 2:23).

How much may depend upon our discerning the mysteries of God in these last days, when the Holy Spirit is doing a quick work upon the earth, in preparing the "handful of grain . . . upon the top of the mountains," whose "fruit" shall be "as Lebanon" (See Psalm 72:16, m.).

Surely, the word is true today:

"Behold, the days come, saith Jehovah, that the plowman shall overtake the reaper, and the treader of grapes him that soweth seed; and the mountains shall drop sweet wine, and all the hills shall melt" (Amos 9:13).

Let us turn to the seed-grain, and see the picture lesson, that in these last days we may intelligently yield to the pierced hand of God and permit His fullest purposes to be fulfilled in us.

Joined to the Lord, one spirit, the grain of wheat awakens to the law of its being, and yields itself to the Son of God for sowing in the earth. It cries to God to make it fruitful at any cost. The purpose of its life begins to dawn upon it. It sees that there is an element of selfishness in being absorbed in its "*own*" advancement, and its "*own*" growth. It shrinks from the possible garnering alone.

The heavenly Husbandman hears the cry of the grain of wheat, prompted by the Divine Spirit, and silently begins to prepare it for the answer to its prayer. He prepares it for the sowing in the ground by gently and imperceptibly detaching and loosening it from the bands that bind it to its nest.

It may appear as if He had not heeded the cry, and the little grain wonders why He does not answer, but the air and sunshine are doing their silent work. The grain is ripening unconsciously to itself, until suddenly it finds itself loosened from its old ties; a hand takes hold of it; it is caught away and dropped down into some spot of earth, dark, lonely, strange.

What has happened?

The little grain of wheat asked for *fruit*, but not for this strange path. Where is the sunshine, the old companions, the old happy experience? *"Where am I? What does it mean?"* cries the lonely grain. *"Am I to be of no more use?"* "Where is my cosy nest, and all that I have been accustomed to in comfortable and congenial surroundings?" "This dark spot of earth, so repulsive, seems to be injuring my nice coat; it was so beautiful in my little nest on the top of the stalk. I was so far away from earth, *so far above all.*" So the little grain speaks within itself.

Presently it is shocked to find its *covering* going to pieces. This is worse than all. So long as it could retain its exterior beauty it would not mind the isolation, the darkness, the apparent uselessness. "Ah me, is this retrogression? What can it be?"

Moreover, it seems like "giving way" to its

surroundings. It is *broken* by them and is not able to guard itself and remain "far above all" as before. It never thought it would be moved by earthly things again.

Meanwhile, the little grain rests on the faithfulness of God. In spite of these strange dealings it knows that He is a faithful God, and will lead it safely by a way that it, the blind one, knows not. It cries with the Psalmist, "I shall yet praise Him who is the health of my countenance, and my God."

Poor little grain! Trampled upon in the dark earth, buried out of sight, ignored, forgotten. This little grain of wheat that was once so admired. How the other members of the group of grains looked up to it, and listened with reverence to all its counsels!

Like one of old it cries, "Unto me men gave ear, and waited, and kept silence at my counsel. . . . They waited for me as for the rain. . . . If I laughed on them, they believed it not. . . . I chose out their way, and sat chief . . . as one that comforteth the mourners. But *now*—!" (Job 29:21–25; 30:1, *KJV*).

Now it is forgotten as it passes into solitude, crying, "I looked for some to take pity, but there was none; and for comforters, but I found none" (Psalm 69:20). Other children of God may "tell of the sorrow of those whom Thou hast wounded" (Psalm 69:26)—

possibly without a burden of intercession, or anguish of heart, or tears, as suffering with others, "which suffer adversity, as being [themselves] also in the body" (Hebrews 13:3, *KJV*).

Buried grain, *say "Yes" to God.* He is answering your prayers.

Maybe you were occupied with your successful service, and with your happy experience in those old days. How little you were able to understand the temptations and the difficulties of the little blades of wheat. How stern you were with those who fell, not "looking to thyself lest thou also [should] be tempted" (Galatians 6:1).

How you talked to the tiny blades of green just peeping through the ground, that they "ought" to be much older, and more matured.

How "weak" you thought them because they were bowed to the ground immediately when some heavy foot trod upon them.

How you discouraged them when they were weak in the faith, and did not "receive them," nor bear lovingly with their weaknesses. How you tried to make them see what you saw in your fuller maturity. You did not understand how to wait, and to encourage them, and to give them time to grow. You wanted to hurry them on, and failed to see that they would have increased vision only as they followed on to "know the

Lord."

Buried grain, you were "verily guilty concerning your brother" in your lack of "anguish of heart and many tears" over the temptations and sorrows of others. How you guarded *yourself*, and feared to stoop down to earth—to become as weak to the weak, that you might gain the more!

Now learn the mystery of the kingdom unfolded in the picture lesson of the grain of wheat, remembering that it is only a picture lesson. The life of God in you *could not break forth into fruitfulness* until *you* had been broken by God's own hand. The earthly surroundings and testings, the loneliness and humiliation, were permitted by Him that He might *release* into life abundant the life that had come from God.

At each stage of growth there must be the casting off of much that was necessary before, if there is to be fuller development. At the beginning, the germ of life is hidden within the outward form of the written word; the shell may pass away (*i.e.*, from our memories) but the life—the Living Word—remains. Under favorable conditions for growth, in "an honest and good heart," cleansed from all that would choke the seed, the life progresses, showing itself in varied outward forms that may be described as the blade, the stalk, the ear, the full grain in the ear.

In the fullness of time the knife must be used, for there must come the severance from old supports, the parting with old experiences, the passing away of outward things that once helped us. The blades of green, the stalk, the head of wheat, were only outward coverings for a life that was *pressing through them to full maturity* and sacrifice for fruitfulness.

Severed from old supports, detached from old surroundings, again the life within the matured grain cannot break forth into the hundredfold without a further stripping—a breaking of an outward shell that would prevent the fruitfulness.

In honest hearts crying out to God for His fullest purposes to be fulfilled in them, the Holy Spirit works even when they do not understand His working. The danger lies in their clinging to old experiences, and old helps, and old supports—when the Spirit-life within is pressing them on to another stage; especially if that stage seems "downward" instead of "upward," although our picture lesson shows us that "downward" means fruitfulness, and is *in the sequence of the "upward" path* of full development of the grain of wheat.

What all this means in practical experience, the Holy Spirit alone can make us understand. It is sufficient for us to know something of the principles of His working, that we may learn to yield trustfully to all His dealings; that we may not "think it strange" when we are *"weighed down exceedingly,"* so that we despair "even of life"—and have as the answer to all our questionings that it is *"death within ourselves, that we should not trust in ourselves, but in God who raiseth the dead"* (2 Corinthians 1:9).

MUCH FRUIT

"Except a grain of wheat fall into the earth and die, it abideth by itself alone; but if it die, it beareth much fruit" (John 12:24).

"Death worketh in us . . . life in you" (2 Corinthians 4:12).

At last the grain of wheat is willing to be hidden away from the eyes of men. Willing to be trampled upon and lie in silence in some lonely corner chosen of God. Willing to appear what others would call a "failure." Willing to live in the will of God apart from glorious experiences. Willing to dwell in solitude and isolation, away from happy fellowship with the other grains of wheat.

The little grain has learned something of the meaning of fellowship with Christ in His death, and now comes to pass the saying: *"Whosoever shall lose his life for My sake shall find it"* (Matthew 16:25).

Silently, surely, the divine life breaks forth into fruitfulness. The grain has given itself, it has parted with its "own life," yet it still lives—*lives now in the life of its Lord.*

A buried seed-grain, it is content to be forgotten! For who thinks of the *grain*, and of all the sorrow and suffering that it underwent while sown in the dark, when they see the harvest field? But the grain of wheat is satisfied, because the law of its being is fulfilled. It has *sunk itself and its own getting*, and now lives in others, not even desiring to have it known that from it the hundredfold has sprung.

So the Christ Himself poured out His soul unto death, that He might "see His seed." See the travail of His soul and be satisfied, as He lives again in His redeemed ones. Thus in God's wondrous law—the law of nature repeated in the spiritual world—the first grain of wheat, sown by God Himself, is reproduced in other grains, having the same characteristics and law of being—"*If it die . . . much fruit.*"

THE LIFE OUT OF DEATH

"If it die, it beareth much fruit. . . . If any man serve Me, let him follow Me; and where I am, there shall also My servant be: . . . him will the Father honor" (John 12:24, 26).

"For ye died, and your life is hid with Christ in God" (Colossians 3:3).

We have followed the little grain in its downward path into the ground to die; it has "hated its life in this world," and now its life is hid with Christ in God.

"Where I am, there shall also My servant be." While it has been consenting to the breaking and stripping in its lonely hidden path, the divine life within it has been breaking forth in life to others, and silently springing up into stronger, fuller, purer union with the Ascended Lord. *"Where I am, there shall also My servant be"*—the servant that will follow Me to My cross and My grave shall go with Me to the Father, and his "life shall abide in heaven" (Philippians 3:20, *Conybeare*). "Where I am, they . . . *with Me"* (John 17:24).

THE FIRST GRAIN OF WHEAT AS THE PATTERN

"Now is My soul troubled; and what shall I say? Father, save Me from this hour. But for this cause came I unto this hour. Father, glorify Thy name" (John 12:27–28).

Even the Lord Christ was troubled as He drew near the hour of desolation and suffering foreshadowed in Psalm 22. The hiding of the Father's face was more than broken heart, than nails and spear. *He could have saved Himself,* He could have spoken to His Father and had legions of angels to fulfill His behests, but where then would have been the first-fruits unto God and the Lamb?

"Now is My soul troubled: and what shall

I say? Father, save Me?" Nay, the Master's only prayer could be—"Father, glorify Thy name."

When Thou dost hide Thy face—
Glorify Thy name.
When Thou art silent to My bitter cry—
Glorify Thy name.
When others reproach and despise Me—
Glorify Thy name.
When I am taunted that God has failed Me—
Glorify Thy name.
When I am poured out like water;
when My heart fails me,
My strength is dried up,
and I am brought to the dust of death—
"Father, glorify Thy name."

If we follow the Lamb whithersoever He goeth, there will surely come to us, as to Him, the assurance from the Father: "I have both glorified it, and will glorify it again."

"He that overcometh, I will give to him to sit down with Me in My throne, as I also overcame, and sat down with My Father in His throne. He that hath an ear, let him hear what the Spirit saith to the churches" (Revelation 3:21–22).

CHAPTER 4

THE HIDDEN LIFE OF
THE GRAIN OF WHEAT

(From the Godward side)

"For ye died, and your life is hid with Christ in God" (Colossians 3:3). "*Where I am, there* shall also My servant be" (John 12:26). "*Where I am*, they . . . with Me" (John 17:24).

GOD is teaching many of His children today the mysteries of the kingdom, as pictures in the seed-grain buried out of sight yet living with Christ in God, in the power of an indissoluble life.

Just so far as they have "hated" their "own life," to share in the life of the Lord, do they taste "the powers of the age to come" (Hebrews 6:5) and have the *earnest* of their inheritance—a handful of the very same life that shall be theirs in all its fullness, when "what is mortal" shall be "swallowed up of life" (2 Corinthians 5:4). United to Christ and hidden in God, they dwell at the source of every precious thing, and in intercession at the Throne exercise even now "authority over the nations," and power "over all the power of the enemy," for "out of the mouth of *babes* . . . hast Thou established strength . . . that Thou mightest still the enemy and the avenger" (Psalm 8:2). They bring forth "much fruit" by abiding in living and hidden union with the Ascended Lord. They hide in Him, while, according to His promise, He abides in them, and glorifies His Father through them, producing fruit that shall remain and bear the test of the fire at the judgment seat.

In Matthew 6 the characteristics of the hidden life in the aspect of prayer are unfolded by Him who was the very embodiment of all He taught.

1. It is prayer with no thought of what others think. Matthew 6:5.

2. It is prayer shut in with God, whether in private or public, for God's hidden ones are in the inner chamber of His presence the moment they approach Him anywhere, and they see and hear none but God. Matthew 6:6.

3. It is prayer not so much of language as of heart. They do not need to use "vain repetitions," for if they know that He *heareth*, they know that they *have* the petitions asked of Him. Matthew 6:7.

4. It is prayer sure of response, for they speak to a Father who knows their need, and, "How much more shall your Father . . . give good things to them that ask Him?" Matthew 6:8.

5. It is prayer *definite and to the point*, for the Son of God knew His Father's heart, and taught His children how few were the words requisite to bring response when He said, "After *this manner* pray ye." Matthew 6:9.

6. It is the prayer of a child to a Father, and in union with the other children: "Our Father . . . in heaven." Matthew 6:9.

7. It is prayer that puts God's glory and God's kingdom first, and before all personal interest: "Hallowed be *Thy* name, *Thy kingdom* come." Matthew 6:9–10.

8. It is prayer with a surrendered will for the will of God to be done in them as implicitly, and as rapidly, as it is done in heaven. Matthew 6:10.

9. It is prayer not for luxuries, but for necessities: "Our bread for the coming day" (m.); which means a life of simplicity, and contentment with "such things as ye have." Matthew 6:11.

10. It is prayer in the spirit of forgiving love: "We also have forgiven our debtors"—

therefore we can ask Thee to forgive us our debts. Matthew 6:12.

11. It is prayer in conscious dependence upon God's keeping and in knowledge of the terrible forces of evil, and the evil one, arrayed against the children of the heavenly Father in the realm of "the world rulers of this darkness." Matthew 6:13.

In short, the hidden life is just the life of a little child, even a little child living in its Father's presence, desiring its Father's will, depending upon its Father for protection from all its foes, and showing its Father's spirit to all around.

Moreover, the soul abiding with Christ in God is given—

"Hidden manna" for the sustenance of the inner life.

"To him that overcometh . . . will I give of the hidden manna" (Revelation 2:17).

"He that eateth Me, he also shall live because of Me" (John 6:57).

"Hidden wisdom" that is withholden from the wise.

"The wisdom of God . . . the hidden wisdom . . . revealed . . . by His Spirit" (1 Corinthians 2:7–10, *KJV*).

"Hid . . . from the wise and prudent, revealed . . . unto babes" (Matthew 11:25, *KJV*).

"Hidden riches" gained only in times of

testing.

"I will give thee the treasures of darkness, and hidden riches of secret places" (Isaiah 45:3).

"I know thy . . . tribulation, . . . but thou art rich" (Revelation 2:9).

Fed with the hidden manna provided at the Father's table alone; taught the hidden wisdom that the princes of this world do not know; given the hidden riches that can only be gained in times of trial and darkness—surely it is true that to them that love God, "God worketh all things with them for good" (Romans 8:28, m.), even to them that He has foreordained to be made like to the image of His Son, the first among many brethren.

Only through the testings can we enter into deep and full life in God. We can only know our God and His abundant grace as He brings us through circumstances that are "a good deal beyond the possible point," as someone once said. Each "impossible" point simply casts us upon the God in whom we hide. "Deep"—"Dwell deep," said Ezekiel the prophet. How can we unless we have no resource but God, no refuge but in Him?

Dwelling deep in the heart of their God, the hidden souls are then—
"Hidden"
from the strife of tongues ....Psalm 31:20.

"Hidden"

   in time of trouble .... Psalm 27:5.

"Hidden"

   from the storm .... Isaiah 4:6.

"Hidden"

   in the secret presence of God ...... Psalm 31:20.

"Hidden"

   under His wings .... Psalm 17:8.

"Hidden,"

   yes, hidden "behind the Lord" .... Psalm 91:1,
                                            Syriac.

These passages tell of a life environed by God Himself, for "in Him we live, and move, and have our being."

Finally, as regards the outward service of these hidden ones: They no longer "run" without being "sent," for their service as well as their life is changed. Their place is now *in the hand of God:* "In the shadow of His hand hath He hid me: and He hath made me a polished shaft; in His quiver hath He kept me close" (Isaiah 49:2).

The souls who are hid with Christ in God are thus under His full control. He keeps them close until the right moment arrives for sending them forth as "polished shafts," silent and sure. When God wields the weapon He strikes the mark, for He knows the spot to aim at in the city of Mansoul.

When not in active use they are kept hidden in His quiver, always ready at His hand. Polished shafts, ah, they need much polishing to get the roughness off them, but the Master Workman knows how to prepare His instruments for His use.

The "polished shafts" are kept for hidden work, awaiting in the sanctuary, entering into the counsels of God, ready to fulfill His will.

"Verily Thou art a God that hidest Thyself" (Isaiah 45:15).

"There was the hiding of His power" (Habakkuk 3:4) tells us that God's deepest work is hidden work. He is preparing a *hidden kingdom*, while permitting the kingdoms of this world to stand until all is ready. "In the days of those kings shall the God of heaven *set up a kingdom* which shall never be destroyed . . . it shall break in pieces and consume all these kingdoms" (Daniel 2:44).

He is also building a *hidden temple*, for a habitation of God through the Spirit, and preparing a *hidden Bride* to share the throne of His Son. Yes, in this dispensation He is still a God that *hideth Himself*, and there is the hiding of His power as He silently works out His purposes, until the day when—

"Christ, who is our life, shall be manifested, then shall [we] also with Him be manifested in glory" (Colossians 3:4).

"How unsearchable are His judgments, and His ways past tracing out" (Romans 11:33).

"*Thou didst hide these things from the wise and understanding, and didst reveal them unto babes*" (Matthew 11:25).

"*Even so, Father: for so it seemed good in Thy sight*" (Matthew 11:26, *KJV*).

"IF IT DIE . . ."

"IF it die," oh, hear the message
  Falling from thy Lord.
"If it die," much fruit it beareth,
  'Tis thy Saviour's word.

Would'st thou see life work in others
  Thou thyself must die.
Fall into the ground, be buried,
  Low in darkness lie.

But He leaves thee not in darkness,
  Light shall greet thine eyes,
And in glad new life and glory
  He shall bid thee rise.

Dost thou crave to tread the pathway
  And His life to share?
As thou passest through death's gateway
  He will meet thee there.

Thou shalt learn the blessed secret:
  He shall live that dies,
From a life poured out in secret
  Shall a harvest rise.

FREDA HANBURY-ALLEN

BOOK 3

THE SILENCE OF JESUS

CONTENTS

FROM DEATH TO LIFE

"LOOK at a grain of wheat not yet fallen to the ground. . . . It is itself, and has itself, and will remain itself: 'it abideth *alone*'; it is 'bare grain.' All it asks for is to be taken care of, lest it be injured and broken. It neither receives nor gives.

"'*Falls into the ground and dies*'—how many Christians are passing through experiences which are filling these words with meaning! Upon the self that encased the heavenly life hostile forces are busily engaged. These forces are of grace. They come from the cross, and are ministered by that Spirit whose prerogative it is to kill and to make alive; but they often reach us in 'the ground' of poverty, trial, ill-health, frustrated schemes, stern providences, and the like. It may seem, at times, as though our spirit were being stripped even to the point of not being 'clothed upon'; *i.e.*, self may be so broken that life appears to have no interest or attraction left. . . .

"But then it is that He who maketh alive begins to clothe us. . . . In the midst of the trying experiences of death, we are conscious that a strange new life is slowly becoming ours. What that new life is, it would be very difficult to describe to those who know it not. The Apostle's words shall suffice: 'To me to live is Christ.' . . . In a sense never dreamt of before, probably, 'all things are ours'; and, in blessedness beyond telling, we 'bring forth fruit *unto God*'—not unto self."

REV. C. G. MOORE
in *Things Which Cannot Be Shaken*

BOOK 3

CHAPTER 1

THE SILENCE OF JESUS

"He opened not His mouth."

"He that saith he abideth in Him ought himself also to walk even as He walked" (1 John 2:6).

"As a lamb that is led to the slaughter, and as a sheep that before its shearers is dumb, so He opened not His mouth" (Isaiah 53:7).

"I WILL dwell in them, and walk in them" (2 Corinthians 6:16) is the promise of God, and only as this promise is fulfilled to the believer can the "silence of Jesus" be known in the daily life. As we trace out the pattern of the walk of Christ on earth so that we may "follow His steps," let us remember that it is not that we may *copy* Him, but rather that we have before us the pattern of the way "the life of Jesus" will be *manifested* in our mortal body as He "walks" in us, and we intelligently yield ourselves to Him to work in us to will and to do of His good pleasure. Let us first note in the pattern of His life—

1. *His Silence over His Blessing of Others*

"He sent him away to his house saying, Neither go into the town nor tell it to any . . ." (Mark 8:26, *KJV*).

"He charged them that they should tell no man" (Mark 7:36).

Was it that He wanted to be hidden and silently to bless and help souls and then pass on? "He shall not strive, nor cry aloud; neither shall anyone hear His voice in the streets" (Matthew 12:19) said the prophet Isaiah of the promised Messiah. The Master's work was so "modest" and done with as little "noise" as possible. It is said of some whom He charged to be silent over what He had done for them that "so much the more they published it," so that His fame went abroad and He was given much trouble to deal with the multitudes. The lesson just for us as to the "silence of Jesus" in this respect is that we should not "publish abroad" the "fame" of the instrument God uses in blessing us, but rather that we tell what the *Lord* has done, and allow His servants to pass on in quiet unobtrusiveness to do His work.

Another lesson in the silence of Jesus we see in—

2. *His Silence in Delicate Difficulties*

"When therefore the Lord knew how that the

Pharisees had heard that Jesus was making
. . . more disciples than John . . . He left
Judea" (John 4:1, 3).

"The Lord knew that the *Pharisees* had
heard. . . ." Reports even came to Him, and
He took trouble to answer these "reports"
by wise action. He could not allow even
apparent rivalry between His great forerunner John the Baptist and Himself, in the
eyes of the religious world. So He simply
and quietly withdrew! The trouble was met
by His silence and His self-effacing action.
So may it be with us to "give no occasion to
the adversary to speak reproachfully." Let
there be wise action in similar circumstances and *silence*, so that others are not
hurt. "In honor preferring one another."

3. *His Silence over the Glory of the Mount*
"He was transfigured before them. . . . As
they were coming down from the mountain, He
charged them that they should tell no man
what things they had seen . . ." (Mark 9:2, 9).

While the Lord Jesus walked on earth as
man, only the three disciples knew of that
glory on the Mount! The world did not
know, neither did the majority of the followers of Jesus, for we are told the chosen
three "kept the saying."

There is a good lesson for us in this
"silence of Jesus" regarding His sacred
hours on the Transfiguration Mount. The

Apostle Paul had learned it when he wrote to the Corinthians concerning the abundance of the revelations given to him by God: "I forbear, lest any man should account of me above that which he seeth me to be . . ." (2 Corinthians 12:6). The reticence of the Bible is very wonderful when we consider it. The veil is lifted off the things of God only just enough to give a glimpse into the unspeakable glory for those who are admitted within the veil. Detailed accounts of God's deepest and most sacred dealings with His children are, if not wrong, at least not wise, lest, as Paul said, we "glory in men" and account them to be "above" what they really are. Again there is also the danger of the "natural man," unable to receive the things of the Spirit, turning away, saying "This is a hard saying," and walking no more with the Lord—stumbled by things he cannot understand. The "silence of Jesus" over the glory of the Mount is a message to all those who know something of the Mount of Transfiguration, to keep God's secrets until God's time comes to make the hidden things manifest to the world.

4. *His Silence over the Path of the Cross*
"The cup that I drink ye shall drink; and with the baptism that I am baptized withal shall ye be baptized . . ." (Mark 10:39).

This was all that He said to the men who asked to share His throne. He did not describe in detail what "drinking the cup" would mean. It would be time enough when they came to it! "Ye cannot bear them now," He tenderly said of the "many things" upon His heart ere He went to Gethsemane. He told them of the *cross*, and that it would mean some cost, but of that path through the valley of deep darkness He was silent.

Let us then co-operate with His restraining hand upon us when He keeps us from exposing too fully the path of the cross, as well as the Mount of Glory. The "glory" would overpower the babes, and so would the way of Calvary. God will lead us all on as we are able to bear it. Let us be tender with the babes, and yet not shrink from faithful speaking when God's time is come.

5. *His Silence over the Traitor Disciple*

"Verily, verily, I say unto you, that one of you shall betray Me. The disciples looked one on another, doubting of whom He spake" (John 13:21–22).

So silent had He been! So lovingly had He treated Judas as one of the rest *that they had no idea who He meant!* Never by word or look had He shown them the traitor. How "displeased" the ten were with the two disciples who asked for the throne (Mark 10:41), so how could the Lord Jesus expose Judas or arouse their partiality, and produce division among His little band? Let us be silent in similar circumstances, and *not arouse partiality* in those who care for us when God is leading us to Calvary through the instrumentality of a Judas. Let us never speak if we can avoid it of the human instruments in the pathway of the cross, nor omit the stooping to wash their feet. To "bless" those who "despitefully use you" (Matthew 5:44, *KJV*) is just what Jesus did!

6. *His Silence over the Deep Things of God*

"These things I said not unto you from the beginning. . . . I have yet many things to say unto you, but ye cannot bear them now" (John 16:4, 12).

"He spake the word unto them, as they were able to hear it" (Mark 4:33).

The power and the need of silence in the spiritual life must have grown upon us as we have followed from point to point the example of the Lord. Silence over the "glory"; silence over the suffering path; and now silence over the things of God which are beyond the stage of growth of others who look to us for help. The Apostle Paul also learned his lesson. "I fed you with milk and not with meat, for ye were not yet able to bear it," he writes again to the Corinthians (1 Corinthians 3:2). To "confess

Christ" is quite a different thing to our forc-
ing "strong meat" on babes.

7. *His Silence over Questions*
"Lord, how?" "In that day ye shall ask Me no
question" (John 14:22, *KJV* and 16:23).

The Lord knew that nothing but practical
teaching by the Holy Spirit could unfold to
these disciples all they wanted to know.
How full of questions we are! "Why?"
"How?" "When?" How we want spiritual
things made clear and plain to our *minds*,
forgetting that God wants to do for us exceeding abundantly above all we can ask
and *think!* How wisely the Lord dealt with
His questioning disciples. The "silence of
Jesus" here is indeed a need for all who are
in the position of teaching others. He only
answered the question with the words, "You
shall know by and by." "The Holy Spirit will
teach you." "Wait." Let us thus leave our
own questions with God, and lead other
questioning hearts to do the same, knowing that in God's time we shall "know" all
He thinks it good for us to know.

8. *His Silence in False Accusation*
"And the chief priests accused Him of many
things. And Pilate again asked Him, saying,
Answerest thou nothing? Behold how many
things they accuse thee of. But Jesus no more
answered anything; insomuch that Pilate mar-
velled" (Mark 15:3–5).

The Apostle Peter writes years afterwards of this wonderful silence of the God-man. "When He was reviled, He reviled not again. When He suffered, He threatened not" (1 Peter 2:23). His silence was divine. No merely human being could have been dumb in this way and, being *innocent and guilt-less,* allow himself to be "led" as a lamb to the slaughter—to be as a sheep dumb in the hand of the shearers. This silence before Pilate and then the silence on the cross in the midst of untold agony—silence only broken seven times with brief words of wonderful meaning—this silence of Jesus was the climax to a life of God-like silence in circumstances when men must speak. A life of silent waiting until thirty years of age before He entered on public ministry and, ultimately, made His lamb-like way to the cross; a life of silence over glory unspeak-able with His Father, and suffering untold at the hands of men; of tender silence over blessing to others, and over Judas' traitor path. This is the pattern for all who would "follow His steps." The pattern for the one who would "walk as He walked," by His walking again in them. And how can it be? Only by seeing the "calling" and accepting it (1 Peter 1:15). And by taking His cross as our cross, "*we having died . . .*" in Him, and with Him, can thus live unto God, and then the silence of Jesus can be known in truth, and we shall be:

"Silent" in our lowly service among others, not seeking to be "seen of men."

"Silent" over the glory of the hours on the Mount, lest others think of us above that which is written.

"Silent" over the depths of the Calvary pathway that led us to God.

"Silent" over the human instruments permitted of God to hand us over to the judgment hall, and the forsaking of our nearest and dearest.

"Silent" while we stood to serve the very ones who have betrayed us.

"Silent" over the deep things of God revealed in the secret place of the Most High, things "impossible to utter" to those who have not yet been "baptized" with that baptism without which they will be "straitened" in spiritual perception "until it is accomplished."

"Silent" over questions only to be answered by God the Holy Spirit, when "that day" dawns for the questioning heart and silences all doubt by the glorious revelation of Him who is the answer to all our need.

"Silent" when forced by others to some position where apparent rivalry with another much-used servant of God seems imminent, only to be hushed by utter self-effacement, and our silent withdrawal without explanation, irrespective of our "rights."

"Silent," yea, "silent" in the judgment hall of our co-religionists, when criticized and falsely accused of many things.

Thou Anointed Christ—the Lamb of God—Thou alone canst live this life of silent self-effacement in a world of self-assertion and self-love. *Live Thou this life in me.*

"These are they which follow the Lamb whithersoever He goeth" (Revelation 14:4).

CHAPTER 2

TAKE IT PATIENTLY

"If, when ye do well, and suffer for it, ye shall take it patiently, this is grace with God" (1 Peter 2:20, m.).

EVEN hereunto were ye called. Called out of darkness into marvelous light to "show forth the excellencies of Him who called you" (1 Peter 2:9). This is the heavenly calling: To be living revelations of Jesus Christ. To endure grief, suffering wrongfully. To "do well . . . suffer for it . . . [and] take it *patiently, this* is grace" (v. 20, m). "*This* is acceptable with God" (v. 20). *This* is thankworthy. Yes, this is the life of Jesus, manifested in our mortal body. This is walking as He walked, so that the Father says, "Thank you."

Look at the pattern given us in the Lord from heaven:

1. *He did no sin* (v. 22)

Yet He was numbered with the transgressors. He could say to His enemies,

"Many good works have I showed you from the Father; for which of those works do ye stone Me?" (John 10:32). They hated Him without a cause. He endured grief, *"suffering wrongfully."*

2. *He had no guile in His mouth* (v. 22)

"Never man spake like this man." "All bare Him witness and wondered at the words of grace which proceeded out of His mouth" (Luke 4:22). Yet—He "suffered wrongfully"!

3. *He did not threaten as He suffered*

"When He suffered, threatened not" (v. 23).

He gave His back to the smiters, He hid not His face from shame and spitting. Holy, harmless and undefiled, He did well, and suffered for it.

He *did* suffer under the reviling. He *did* feel the pain of the reproach. He *did* feel the taunts, and the humiliation laid upon Him. He said, "Reproach hath broken My heart" (Psalm 69:20). He knew that an awful visitation lay before the ones who said, "His blood be on us and on our children," yet He was dumb, He threatened not.

4. *He silently committed all to God*

"He . . . committed Himself to Him that judgeth righteously" (v. 23).

"Committed His cause" (margin). To Him it was "the cup which the Father hath given

Me." "Why not rather take wrong?" said Paul the Apostle to the Corinthians! Why indeed, with such a calling and such a Pattern.

How often we have fled away to some place alone with God to shed bitter tears over some "battle of words" and "strife of tongues" that would have been avoided had we learned the grace of suffering wrongfully.

How is this grace possible to men and women in this present evil world?

Taking heed that we give "no occasion" to suffer *rightfully*, let us see how clearly the apostle gives us the secret of deliverance from the self-vindication and self-defence so contrary to the spirit of the Lamb.

"Who His own self carried up our sins in His body to the tree, that we, *having died* unto sins, might live unto righteousness; by whose stripes ye were healed" (v. 24, margin).

Peter knew the power of the cross, even as did his "beloved brother Paul." He had actually been a witness of the sufferings of Christ (1 Peter 5:1). How vividly he could depict the Pattern; how his heart must have quivered as he remembered that denial of his Lord in the house of Caiaphas, when the meek and lowly One had been "wounded" by one of His friends! How the tears must have come, as he remembered that all the Master had given him in return was one look of love—*one look!* One look that broke his heart. Yes, Peter knew Calvary, and turned from the Pattern to show the secret of the life of enduring grief, suffering wrongfully, in the words—

"His own self carried up our sins . . . to the tree, that we, *having died . . .*"

with Him who died, might follow in His steps (1 Peter 2:24, m.).

In the next chapter we see the blessed outcome of a life thus lived. See it in the special case of wives with unbelieving husbands, but surely applicable to every relationship of life:

"*In like manner,* ye wives, be in subjection to your own husbands; that . . . they may *without the word* be gained by the manner of life of their wives" (1 Peter 3:1, m.).

"In like manner," ye sisters, win your brothers. "If I could but get _____ to hear the gospel," we often hear it said, but Peter tells us the loved ones can be won "without the word."

"Won" by taking patiently all contradiction, all suffering wrongfully.

So shall come upon the earthen vessels the heavenly adornment of a "meek and quiet spirit"—in the sight of God of great price.

So may it be for His glory. Amen.

CHAPTER 3

THE BLESSED "UNOFFENDED"

"Blessed is he, whosoever shall not be offended in Me" (Matthew 11:6).*

JOHN THE BAPTIST is in prison for righteousness sake. The lonely prisoner hears of the works of Christ, and he who had once borne witness to Him as the Anointed One of God sends two of his disciples to Him with a question that reveals how the iron had entered his soul, as, apparently forsaken of God, he ponders over the past, and in a moment of overwhelming perplexity the terrible doubt enters his mind whether the One he had testified to as the Son of God was the Messiah after all.

"*Art thou He that should come, or do we look for another?*" was the brief message to the Lord (v.3).

Could these words really come from him who had so boldly said: "*I saw, and bare*

---

* References in this chapter are from the *KJV*.

record that this is the Son of God" (John 1:34)?

Taught of the Spirit, John had also said, "He must increase but *I must decrease*" (John 3:30). He was the Forerunner of the Christ, and must of necessity pass out of sight as his work was done, so that all attention should be focused upon Him whose herald he was. But the Holy Spirit withheld the knowledge as to how the "decreasing" would come about, and he did not dream that his path of service would end in imprisonment, and a martyr's death.

"Was I mistaken after all?" we can think of John saying to himself one day in his prison. "Was it the Messiah, or only a great prophet, and has Israel yet to look for another as the promised One?"

The messengers are sent, and in answer to John's brief question the Lord Jesus bids them return to him and simply tell him what their eyes had seen. John was doubtless well acquainted with the writings of the prophet Isaiah, and his disciples could now tell him that the Spirit of God was manifestly upon the Prophet of Galilee. They saw the blind receiving their sight, the lame walking, the lepers being cleansed, the deaf hearing, and the poor needy souls having glad tidings preached to them.

"Tell John the things which ye do hear

and see," said Jesus to John's disciples; and this was all the answer He deemed necessary to send to the lonely prisoner. Yet He adds, in tender significant words, a brief personal message for his heart's need—a message that would serve as an anchor to John's faith in the still deeper suffering that the Master knew lay yet before him: "Tell John . . . Blessed is he, whosoever shall not be offended in Me" (Matthew 11:6).

It is as if the Christ would say to His sorely tried servant, "I am meeting the needs of others, but *your* need is not forgotten, John! I have reserved a special blessing for you. Something far higher than anything I am bestowing upon these around Me. An eternal blessedness far beyond any deliverance from *present* trial and *present* suffering; the special blessing reserved for those who will not be offended with Me, however strangely I may deal with them; even though, while delivering others, I leave them in prison, darkness, loneliness, suffering, death, that their faith may be found unto honor at My appearing."

No word of rebuke did the Lord send to His tempted Forerunner. He knew that "all chastening *seemeth* for the present to be not joyous, but grievous," and so He sent the message to lift his faith to the "*afterward*" of the peaceable fruit for eternity.

Did John whisper, "*Not offended, Lord,*" on that still darker day when the devil apparently triumphed, and God's faithful servant was hurried to a martyr's death? "Not [having been given] deliverance," that he might "obtain a better resurrection," even a martyr's crown!

When the disciples of John had departed with their message, Jesus turns to the multitude and bears witness to John, even as John had once borne witness to Him on the banks of Jordan:

"This is he of whom it is written, Behold, I send My messenger. . . . There hath not risen a greater than John the Baptist" (Matthew 11:10–11).

So "great" was John that he could be trusted not only with public "successful" service but with prison and suffering, without any explanation from the Lord; trusted to go to a humiliating death with only a brief message from the Christ to whom he had witnessed so well.

Jesus testified of John that he was "a burning and a shining light" at the *very time* that he sends the message revealing what sore trial and perplexity he was in. Even in prison he was a "shining light" to his God—a light burning all the more brightly for the darkness of his surroundings.

The Master knew the loyal heart, and knew that the brief message bidding him not be offended with the strange silence and dealings of his Lord would be sufficient to draw out the faith that asks no deliverance from present suffering, but in the hour of trial cries:

"What shall I say? Father, save me from this hour? . . . Father, glorify Thy name" (John 12:27–28).

The word "whosoever" in the Master's message to John shows that the blessing promised to him, if he would not be offended with his Lord for leaving him apparently undelivered, is a blessing open to every child of God who will follow in his steps. "Blessed is he"—not only John the Baptist, but—"*whosoever* shall not be offended in Me."

That we may share in the special blessing promised to John and opened to us by the word "whosoever," let us turn to other passages of Scripture, and learn how to be "unoffended" today.

Let us note first that Isaiah clearly prophesied that the Messiah when He came would be a "Rock of offence":

"He shall be for a Sanctuary . . . and for a Rock of offence . . . and many among them shall stumble" (Isaiah 8:14–15).

"Not offended IN ME" was the Master's

message to John, and His words interpret the passage in Isaiah.

Christ is to every soul either a "Sanctuary" or a "Rock of offence." We either take refuge in Him and learn to know His heart so as to be "unoffended" with Him, or else we resent His claims, His way of salvation, His cross, His will, His dealings with us, and, in short, find Him continually a rock of offence in our path. He is a "stone of stumbling and a rock of offence" to the *disobedient* (1 Peter 2:8), but to those who believe and hide in Him, He is precious.

In the Gospels we find the description of some who found the Lord a rock of offence, and in them we may see depicted some points in our own lives where we may become offended, cast away our confidence, and lose our reward.

1. *The Offended Converts*

"He that heareth . . . [and] with joy receiveth, . . . when *tribulation* or *persecution* ariseth . . . is offended" (Matthew 13:20–21).

These souls received the word of life with joy, but when they were tested by tribulation (or, *the threshing*) and the heavenly Husbandman began to separate the chaff from the wheat in their lives, they were "offended."

They had not counted the cost of following Christ. Joy, peace, prosperity, all this they had expected—but no cross.

"Christ bore the cross *that we might be free from a cross*," we hear again and again from those who bear His name.

Yes, He suffered *for* us that He might bring us to God, and He alone was the propitiation for our sins, and the sins of the whole world; *but* there is a taking of His cross, a fellowship (*partnership*) with His sufferings clearly put before His children— a fellowship that is to conform us to His image, and be the necessary preparation for our sharing His throne.

"If we suffer, we shall also *reign with Him*," and we are "heirs of God, and joint-heirs with Christ; *if so be* that we suffer with Him, that we may be also glorified together" (Romans 8:17).

For this path of fellowship with Christ in His cross, many converts have not been prepared, and when the "tribulation" begins they are "offended."

2. *The Offended People*

"His own country . . . Is not this the carpenter . . . are not his sisters here with us? And *they were offended at Him!*" (See Mark 6:1–6).

Beholding the carpenter, the son of Mary, they missed the Christ, the Son of God; and "He could there do no mighty work because of their unbelief." The Christ is often today a "rock of offence" in the way

He is pleased to approach men, and in the instruments He deigns to use for their salvation.

He draws near to souls in lowly guise that He may prove who are truly seeking Him, for when we are thirsty for Him we do not care what vessel He uses to satisfy our thirst. We do not quarrel with the "manner" or "expression" of His messengers sent to minister the word of life. "That which was a temptation [trial] to you in my flesh ye despised not, nor *rejected*; but ye received me . . . as Christ Jesus" (Galatians 4:14, *ASV*) wrote the Apostle Paul to the Galatians (Compare 2 Corinthians 10:1–10).

3. *The Offended Formalists*

"This people . . . honoureth Me with their lips; but their heart is far from Me. But *in vain* do they worship Me. . . . The Pharisees *were offended*" (Matthew 15:8–9, 12).

The Christ was a "rock of offence" to the religious formalists of that day, because He told them the truth. They professed to worship His Father, but they were "offended" because He told them that God wanted the worship of the heart, and not merely a profession of the lips. He was a still greater offence in saying that such exterior religion was in vain.

When the Faithful Witness deals thus with us, His own children, and strips all away that He sees to be artificial in our religious life, are we also "offended" with Him?

How few of the followers of Christ really crave to know the bare truth about themselves! Blessed is he who is not offended with his Lord as He slowly and tenderly unveils the hideous life of self, and does not pause until He has brought him to the dust of death, crying, "In me dwelleth no good thing. I am a sinful man, O Lord."

4. *The Offended Disciples*

"He that eateth Me, even he shall live by Me. . . . His disciples murmured. . . . [Jesus] . . . said . . . *Doth this offend you?* From that time many of His disciples went back, and walked no more with Him" (John 6:57, 61, 66).

The Lord Jesus was a "rock of offence" even to some of His disciples. They murmured at the expression of the deep mysteries of God from His lips; were "offended" and left Him because they could not understand His "teaching."

"The words that I speak unto you, they are *spirit*, and they are *life*," said Christ about the strange language of eating His flesh and drinking His blood. If His hearers had but hidden His words in their hearts and waited, the Holy Spirit would have guided them into all the truth, but they were "offended," went back, and walked no more with Him.

So do many of us today foolishly thrust from us heavenly blessings. We are so quickly "offended" with any truth we do not readily grasp or understand.

We measure all things by our present capacity and apprehension, instead of meekly receiving the Word of God, and counting upon the Holy Spirit to bear witness, and bring the seed of the Word into full fruition in His own time and way.

5. *The Offended Inner Circle*

"Then saith Jesus unto them, *All ye shall be offended because of Me*" (Matthew 26: 31).

"Peter answered . . . *Though all shall be offended* . . . yet will I *never be offended.* . . . Likewise also said all the disciples" (Matthew 26: 33–35).

As the Lord drew near the hour for which He had come into the world, He tells His little band that they too would now be offended because of Him. He knew them as they did not know themselves. His words aroused their vehement protestations, but it was written afterwards, "They all forsook Him and fled."

The *offence of the cross* has not yet ceased! We too may fail the Master where His inner circle failed Him long ago!

We may have stood the test when the "threshing" began, and held fast the confession of our faith without wavering; we may have had vision to see the Lord, and hear His voice through any instrument He has chosen to send to us; we may have welcomed the keen edge of His truth, and humbled ourselves under the mighty hand of God; we may have learned to hide His Word in our hearts, and not been "offended" as we have followed Him in the way; all this may be true, and yet—when the real fellowship of His cross is at hand, we may fail Him as Peter did that night in the judgment hall.

"Blessed is he, whosoever shall not be offended in Me" is peculiarly a message for this present time. We are living in solemn days, and there is a deep sense upon many of the nearness of the Lord's appearing.

The *living* members of Christ are being *proved by fire*. All that will "abide the fire" is being made to go "through the fire" (Numbers 31:23).

There is a silent power at work in the professing Church, separating unto God and the Lamb all who are truly joined to Him.

The call to the cross is the touchstone; *the path of the cross the test.* Once more the Christ is saying, *"He that taketh not his cross, and followeth after Me, is not worthy of Me."*

Who among us will follow the Lamb and be "unoffended" souls?

The Lord Himself foretold that many who profess His name would be "offended" in the last days.

"Many shall come in My name, saying, I am Christ; and shall deceive many. And ye shall hear of wars . . . famines . . . pestilences. . . . All these are the beginning of sorrows . . . and ye shall be hated . . . and *then shall many be offended,* and shall betray one another" (See Matthew 24:5–10).

The "*offence* of the cross" must grow more acute as the days go by. The world must turn upon the living members of Christ. Those who reject the cross and its message of salvation through the death of Another, and its call to follow Him in His path of sacrifice, must reject and hate those who glory in the cross and know nothing among men but Jesus Christ crucified. Then— "*shall many be offended.*" But—"*Blessed* is he, whosoever shall not be offended" with God or his brother in the days of the beginning of sorrows.

6. *The Unoffended Followers of the Lamb*
"These things have I spoken unto you, that ye should *not be offended*" (John 16:1).

The unveiling of ourselves, our weakness, failure and sin, is always accompanied with the message of the divine provision to meet our need.

At the supper table the Lord had said,

"All ye shall be offended because of Me this night," but before they parted—He to go to His cross and passion, and they to their shame and sorrow—He unfolded to them the divine secret that would enable them to be "unoffended" when He would be taken from them, and they would be left to bear His name, and be hated of all men for His sake (John 15:18).

Briefly the Master promised them:

The gift of the Holy Ghost the Comforter.

"I will pray the Father, and He shall give you another Comforter" (John 14:16).

The manifestation of Himself as the Risen One.

"I will . . . manifest Myself to [you]" (John 14:18–21).

The knowledge of God the Father.

"My Father will love him, and WE will come . . . and make OUR abode with him" (John 14:20–23).

The Holy Spirit as the Comforter would make real to them the things of Christ, would communicate to them the mind of Christ, would impart to them the life of Christ, and fill them with the peace and joy of Christ.

A soul comforted by the Indwelling Comforter will not be an "offended" soul!

In their walk in the comfort of the Holy

Ghost, the Risen Christ would reveal Himself to them, and they would rejoice in being made partakers of His sufferings that they might be partakers of the glory.

A soul in close fellowship with the Risen Lord will not be an "offended" soul.

In their walk in implicit obedience to His revealed will, Christ would tell them plainly of the Father, and they would know the Father as indwelling them, through the Son, by the Holy Ghost.

A soul that has learned to know the Father will not be an "offended" soul!

"Blessed," with the blessing of God the Father, God the Son, and God the Holy Ghost, is he "whosoever shall not be offended in Me."

Before we close, let us briefly notice the characteristics of unoffended souls in their life in this present evil world:

Unoffended with God or man, they are *"sincere and without offence"* (Philippians 1:9–10), for in deep humility and love they seek to give *"no offence in anything,* that the ministry be not blamed" (2 Corinthians 6:3).

They walk in wisdom to them that are without, as the Master did, *"lest we should offend"* (Matthew 17:27).

They gladly sacrifice even lawful things for the sake of others, lest in any way they become *"offended . . . or made weak"* (Romans 14:21).

In dealing with their own lives they un-flinchingly cast aside all that causes them to "*offend*" (Matthew 18:8–9), for they know that the Master said:

"Woe unto the world *because of offences!* for it must needs be that *offences* come; but woe to that man *by whom the offence cometh!*" (Matthew 18:7).

Those who are offended with the claims of the cross of Christ become "offences" or "stumbling-blocks" in the way of others.

What a sorrowful word for a needy world: "*It must needs be* that offences come." Woe to the world because of offences, the poor world turning from God because of His un-Godlike children.

God grant us grace to be among the unoffended, and save us from the woe of those through whom the offences come.

"Great peace have they which love Thy [will]: and NOTHING shall offend them" (Psalm 119:165).

CHAPTER 4

THE OUTWORKINGS OF THE TRANSFORMED LIFE

Romans 12:9–21*

"Let love be without hypocrisy."   ver. 9.
   Concerning love be genuine.

"Abhor that which is evil; cleave to that which is good."   ver. 9.
   Hate sin, and don't trifle with it.

"Be tenderly affectioned one to another; in honor preferring one another."   ver. 10.
   Give others the first place; be kind and courteous.

"Not slothful in business; fervent in spirit; serving the Lord."   ver. 11, KJV
   "Let our people also learn to profess honest occupations for necessary wants" (Titus 3:14, m.), said Paul, and he did not hesitate, apostle though he was, to work with his own hands that he might not be burdensome to the Corinthians (2 Corinthians 11:9). This dignifies the "honest occupations," and shows that the Lord may be served fervently in business, as well as by preaching the gospel.

---

*References are from the *ASV*.

"Rejoicing in hope; patient in tribulation; continuing stedfastly in prayer."   ver. 12.
This is applicable to business life as well as all other circumstances, and is to be the spirit in which all trials are met: hopeful, patient, prayerful.

"Communicating to the necessities of the saints; given to hospitality."   ver. 13.
Caring for others in the household of faith (see 1 John 3:17) and generous in hospitality (see 3 John ver. 5, 6, 7).

"Bless them that persecute you; bless, and curse not. Rejoice with them that rejoice; weep with them that weep. Be of the same mind one toward another."   ver. 14–16.
Do not retaliate, but conquer with love. Be sympathetic, glad to see others happy, and tender with their griefs. Seek the unity of the Spirit with all.

"Set not your mind on high things."   ver. 16.
Be willing to be among the "nobodies."

"Be contented with mean things."   ver.16, KJV, m.
Be thankful for everything that comes (Psalm 34:13).

"Be not wise in your own conceits."   ver. 16.
Don't think you know everything!

"Render to no man evil for evil."   ver. 17.
Don't pay back people in "their own coin."

"Take thought for things honorable in the sight of all men."   ver. 17.
Think of how things look to others!

"As much as in you lieth, be at peace with all men."   *ver. 18.*

Be peace-makers, not peace-breakers. Refuse to touch the "bone of contention" at home, and in the church.

"Avenge not yourselves . . . give place unto the wrath of God."   *ver. 19, m.*

Beware of self-defence. Hush! Not a word! Remember Luke 18:7.

"If thine enemy hunger, feed him; if he thirst, give him to drink; for in so doing thou shalt heap coals of fire upon his head. Be not overcome of evil, but overcome evil with good." *ver. 20–21.*

Those who hate you, do the most for, and melt an opposition with the fire of heavenly love (Matthew 5:44–45).